Programming Myco/TPS
simulate and run code on Arduino

Learning Programming easily - independent of a PC
Like Memory for Coding

Second Edition
now with more Features included.
Chapters 0 to 8 are identical to the eBook version

Free Simulator for download
Online Simulator planned
Online Assembler planned

Prepared to download Code into ARDUINO
ARDUINO Source Code included

Alternative: Forth Code for TI MSP430G2553

By Juergen Pintaske
A combined Project
and many People involved, mainly

Burkhard Kainka
Wilfried Klaas
Michael Kalus

A first Kit Holtek Chip based, now Simulator Options and Arduino based

This Book is Copyright © ExMark, 15 November 2018

The current Forth Bookshelf can be found at
https://www.amazon.co.uk/Juergen-Pintaske/e/B00N8HVEZM
All are available as eBook – the ones with P after the number as well as print book.

1 Charles Moore - Forth - The Early Years: Background information about the beginnings of this Computer Language
2P Charles Moore - Programming A Problem Oriented Language: Forth - how the internals work
3 Leo Brodie - Starting Forth -The Classic
4P Leo Wong – Juergen Pintaske – Stephen Pelc FORTH LITE TUTORIAL: Code tested with free MPE VFX Forth, SwiftForth and Gforth or else
5P Juergen Pintaske – A START WITH FORTH - Bits to Bites Collection – 12 Words to start, then 35 Words, Javascript Forth on the Web, more
6P Stephen Pelc - Programming Forth: Version July 2016
7P Brad Rodriguez - Moving Forth / TTL CPU / B.Y.O. Assembler
8 Tim Hentlass - Real Time Forth

9P Chen-Hanson Ting - Footsteps In An Empty Valley issue 3
10P Chen-Hanson Ting - Zen and the Forth Language: EFORTH for the MSP430G2552 from Texas Instruments
11 Chen-Hanson Ting - eForth and Zen - 3rd Edition 2017: with 32-bit 86eForth v5.2 for Visual Studio 2015
12P Chen-Hanson Ting - eForth Overview
13 Chen-Hanson Ting - FIG-Forth Manual Document /Test in 1802 IP
14 Chen-Hanson Ting - EP32 RISC Processor IP: Description and Implementation into FPGA – ASIC tested by NASA
15 Chen-Hanson Ting – Irriducible Complexity
16P Chen-Hanson Ting - Arduino controlled by eForth

17 Burkhard Kainka - Learning Programming with MyCo: Learning Programming easily - independent of a PC (Forth code to follow soon)
17bP Burkhard Kainka – Extended Version Programming with MyCo: **Simulator options - Arduino** –source code, Tiny84 - Forth code MSP430G2553
18 Burkhard Kainka - BBC Micro:bit: Tests Tricks Secrets Code, Additional MicroBit information when running the Mecrisp Package
19 Burkhard Kainka – Thomas Baum – Web Programming ATYTINY13
20P Georg Heinrichs – The ATTINY Project – Why Forth ?

Contents

0 Background 8

1 Introduction 10

2 Hardware tests 19

2.1 The basic structure 19

2.2 Two flashing LEDs 21

2.3 Counter combined with PWM 22

2.4 The Analog-to-Digital converter 28

2.5 Random number generator 30

2.6 Pulse length measurement 32

3 The programming mode 35

3.1 Reading out programs 35

3.2 Programming new functions 39

3.3 Back to factory status 42

4 MyCo instructions 43

4.1 The basic instructions 43

4.2 Calculations using Variables 48

4.3 Jumps and Skips 51

4.4 The instruction table 57

5 Program structures and sample programs 58

5.1 Counting loops 58

5.2 Compare instructions 60

5.3 Single bit processing 61

5.4 Basic logic functions 66

5.5 Subroutines 69

6 Advanced applications 72

6.1 Twilight switch 72

6.2 Two-point controller 73

6.3 LED dimmer 75

6.4 Morse code program 77

6.5 Start / Stop timer 80

6.6 Combination lock 82

7 The inner workings of MyCo 86

8 Appendix 89

8.1 Listings of sample programs 89

8.2 Instruction table 97

8.3 Programming model A, B, C 97

8.4_Circuit diagram 98
8.5_Function symbol 99
8.6_PCB with components 99
8.7_Header connectors SV1 and SV2 100
8.8_Hexadecimal table 101
8.9_Holtek processor block diagram 102
8.10_Breadboard 103
8.11_Resistor colors 103
8.12_Flow diagram symbols 104
8.13_Extension via PC Control Interface - Profilab 105
8.14_Circuit digram, Instruction Table 107
8.15_Programming pages 109
8.16_Links 111
8.17_MyCo_in_FORTH_MicroBox_Example 112

9.___Arduino Simulator and Interface to Arduino 113
9.1_The Simulator and first row of Buttons 115
9.2_The Function Window 116
9.3_Instruction Table 117
9.4_TPS/SPS Emulator 118
9.5_ARDUINO GOES TPS 120
9.6_Instruction Tables 124
9.7_Download and ARDUINO Source Code 127
9.8_Holtek and Arduino version Instruction Tables 158

10.___TPS written in FORTH for TI MSP430G2553 160
11.___ATTINY 84 on solderless Breadboard 191
12.___Is Programming really that difficult? - Basics 193

4 Pages duplicated to be cut out as reference 201

Version MycoBook v26b print updated and extended 2018_11_15

A few first Words for this extended Version 2

First: There are some very basic explanations in chapter 12, page 193 to get started.

Burkhard Kainka had a great idea: he defined a microcontroller kit, where a lot of the complexity has been taken out, and all you need is the controller in the middle,
4 Inputs 2 analog Inputs 4 LED outputs
1 additional Output to simulate an analog output voltage.
All you need to program and control this little PLC (Programmable Logic Controller) unit are are 3 pushbuttons.
No PC required.
This first version is available from 3 sources as different setups:
from Franzis Verlag to learn programming and use the kit as a controller, but a lot has happened since it appeared.
There is as well a kit you can buy from Conrad – no soldering required, built via a solderless breadboard.
And the pre-programmed chip is abailable from AK-Modul.
Many people like this minimalistic approach, so many additional little applications are available via Burkhard's website.
An additional option was prepared by Wilfried Klass, where he made a Simulator availabe, where you can program and execute the same functionality – but no kit required.
But, seeing the real LED flash, or add the PLC to tou model train or model board would be nice. Wilfried built this simulator for his own models – and for anybody who is interested.
The next step, leading to this second edition, was his work to couple the Simulator with external hardware and transfer the tested program. ARDUINO is the chosen hardware, as there are probably 1 million or more out there already many probably unused– so a nice target and no extra hardware required.
An additional option is then to take the chip out of the Arduino board, add what is needed in your application around and stick a new chip into the Arduino board.
I am a big fan of the computer language Forth. It is not so well known, but follows the minimalistic approach as well. There is a whole Forth Bookshelf for people who are interested.
And it is interactive, so you can modify the program on the fly. Michael Kalus was very kind and wote an emulator of the TPS/MyCo functionality in Forth. It runs on a Texas Instrments MSP430G2553 chip and includes as well a serial interface function.

As result you can control the program on the chip either via the 3 buttons as before – or from your PC and kann display a lot of the internal status. See Chapter 10.
And as last point in Chapter 11: PROGRAMMING. How difficult is it really? Well, you do it every day without thinking about it.
I have chosen as first example a simplified making coffee using this controller and instructions. Just try to extend this using the other instructions, it should not be too difficult.
Oh, before I forget, in German the name is TPS; I could not find a good meaning for these 3 letters in English, so I just calld it MyCo – my controller, as it will be in your hand.
Enjoy reading. November 2018 version 21

Link to eBook – for now without extensions: https://www.amazon.co.uk/Learning-Programming-MyCo-easily-independent-ebook/dp/B00K6N87UG/ref=asap_bc?ie=UTF8
Link to Franzis Kit - and downloadable part of English eBook
http://www.elektronik-labor.de/Lernpakete/TPS/HandbuchTPS.htm
Link to Conrad Kit and documentation, many more examples
http://www.elektronik-labor.de/Lernpakete/TPS/TPS0.html
Link to AK-Modul for the Holtek Chip
http://www.ak-modul-bus.de/stat/ht46f47e_mit_tps_firmware.html
Link to Forth Bookshelf this book is part of
https://www.amazon.co.uk/Juergen-Pintaske/e/B00N8HVEZM
Link to A Start With Forth data on Forth-ev.de
https://wiki.forth-ev.de/doku.php/en:projects:a-start-with-forth:start0
Link to Burkhard Kainka's website and TPS for ATMEGA8
https://wiki.forth-ev.de/doku.php/en:projects:a-start-with-forth:start0
And Most Important: Link to the Wilfried Klaas website regarding TPS
http://wkla.no-ip.biz/ArduinoWiki/doku.php?id=arduino:arduinosps:spsemu
The TPS Assembler
http://wkla.no-ip.biz/ArduinoWiki/doku.php?id=arduino:arduinosps:tpsass
Link to part of the book for download and print related to Forth mainly
https://wiki.forth-ev.de/doku.php/en:projects:myco:start

A few Words regarding the earlier eBook version:

First, I have to say thank you to the many people who helped to make this eBook happen, and just to mention a few:
Burkard Kainka, the genius behind the German kit who started me on this venture, which proved a lot more time consuming that expected.
Franzis Electronic Kits who sent me some kits immediately, so I could take my own photographs and to let others play with the kit and give feedback.
And my family:
PPP - Patrick Pintaske Photography helped with some of the pictures and editing;
Lisa Pintaske with art help and advice;
My wife Barbara, the one to help, check the book, correct and add her own inputs.
Ralf Lieb and Michael Schwope with feedback and inputs for future extensions, e.g. the build of a board shown in later chapters.

Copyright Dipl.-Ing. Juergen Pintaske, ExMark, May 2014v17
All product names mentioned here are under the copyright of the relevant company or copyright owner.
We have taken great care to ensure that all of the drawings are correct. We appreatiate feedback to epldfpga@aol.com to enable us to correct further editions of this eBook.

This eBook is the description of an existing kit as seen on the cover page. We denounce any liability regarding build and use of it, or for damages that might arise when used in applications.
This is an educational device to be used as is, connecting it to aditional external components could be dangerous.

0 – Background to this Book

When I saw this little kit on the Internet and read what it can do, I could not believe it. A complete computer that you can program, including keyboard and display, input and output. No PC required. Yes, the absolute minimum, but it works. Looking at the low cost and having a bit of fun, was definitely worth the time and the money. You will have to solder the pieces together, but there should always be somebody around who can help if needed. And I assume soon you will be able to buy and sell the kits on eBay already soldered together – ready to go.
If you look at pictures 1, 2 and 3 on the cover page, you see the original box it came in and the little PCB with the Microcontroller on it. There are additional parts included to start you off with the first experiments using pre-programmed code. No need to learn programming first. To make life easier for me afterwards, I soldered wires on to the relevant pins while doing the soldering, to be prepared for later experiments. In this way the hardware would be ready, I just plug this additional new extension connector into the breadboard, and add the components for the experiment - no more soldering.

And the kit worked first time. A wonderful learning toy, I assume the age range could be about 5 to 95. Having gone through the examples, you will understand the basic workings and structure of a computer and as well you can do a little of your own programming. And kids can use it to add functions to their toys – all under software control. I will soon give the kit to some of my neighbors who are teachers, asking for feedback about what the kids think having played with it.
As I live in the UK now, it all has to be in English for them, but this kit is only available in German at the moment. So I decided to write my first eBook.

To give the English-speaking community the chance to relate to the German booklet that comes with the kit, I tried to keep the sequence the same. The name of the kit in German is TPS (roughly translated Switch Programming System), but the designer Burkhard Kainka allowed me to give it my own name. There was a short christening, and MyCo was born - My little Computer.
I hope you have fun reading this eBook, and if you are brave, you might even order the German Kit - I got mine via Amazon within 3 days, build it and enjoy. All of the information in the German booklet and more is in this eBook. To help with your first programming even without having the kit, I generated the Programming Page in the Appendix. Fill in your program and see how the data flows, writing code and data into the relevant boxes. All of the programs in this eBook are identical. Even many of

the pictures. If some of the information seems to be too difficult, you can continue with the examples and go back later.

There is a lot more that has happened around this little kit in the meantime, so there might be another eBook later. Any feedback please to epldfpga@aol.com. Your own programs or applications you can forward to us, including please the ok to publish it on our website or in another eBook; if there is time, we will keep a MyCo area on our website, have a look. Some more information you will find on our website www.exemark.com. Enjoy.

1 - Introduction

This little controller consists of the same functions that you would find in your PC or tablet, just simplified to the extreme. To make it sound big: you get a computer with a minimum keyboard, a minimum display, the minimum central processor with its integrated memory, inputs and outputs, and a programmer for the unit is thrown in for free.

The description of our MyCo functionality is straightforward: there are four digital inputs E1 to E4 and four digital outputs A1 to A4. Additionally, you have two analog inputs AD1 and AD2, and a quasi-analog PWM output that can be extended to a digital-to-analog converter function via an RC low pass.

The reset input of the controller is connected to the reset switch and sets the internal program counter back to starting the program at location 00. The other 2 buttons are for defining a number and for programming – or as two additional inputs. The unit is supplied with a battery case for three AA cells giving you approximately 4.5 V and the kit can work within a range of 2.2V to 5.5V, so 2 AAA cells are ok as well, and this is what I use. In a next step I want to replace them with one rechargeable Li-Ion cell which supplies about 3.5V, and MyCo can be solar powered or at least recharged. Another option would be to use 2 rechargeable NMH cells, often used in wireless handsets.

Specification:

Microcontroller:	Holtek HT46F47
Clock frequency:	about 2 MHz
Internal EEPROM:	128 Bytes
Power supply voltage:	2.2 V to 5.5 V
Current consumption:	about 1 mA at 4.5 V
4 output pins:	support up to 10 mA
1 PWM output:	supports up to 10 mA
4 input lines:	internal resistor sets to 1
2 analog inputs:	0 V ... Vcc
2 switch inputs:	internal resistors set it to 1

Components in this learning package:

1 PCB
1 Holtek HT46F47 pre-programmed with TPS firmware
1 IC socket
3 Push buttons
4 LEDs 3 mm, red - short wire cathode (into square PCB hole)
1 LED 3 mm, green - short wire cathode (into square PCB hole)
1 LDR - Light Dependant Resistor
1 Piezo transducer
3 Capacitors 100 nF
1 Polarised capacitor 47 uF
5 Resistors 2.2 kOhm - red red red plus other colors
1 Resistor 10 kOhm - brown black orange plus other colors
1 Resistor 27 kOhm - red violet orange plus other colors
2 Resistors 100 kOhm - black brown yellow plus other colors
1 Wire 1m
1 Battery compartment with wires, for 3 AA batteries

To program your own code into MyCo, you just need the two buttons S1 and S2, the 4 LEDs at the outputs A1 to A4, plus reset. This little computer is programmed via a total of 14 instructions which are either combined with data or subcommands. Each instruction is a number between 0 and 15, which is 0 to F in hexadecimal, and is combined with 4 bit data as well, so both are 4 bit wide numbers in the range 0000 to 1111 (decimal 0 to 15) and are directly visible on the display LEDs. The actual number for programming is set by pushing S1 n times. Using S2, you change between command and data and increment to the next address for the next instruction. So each instruction consists of 2 nibbles of 4 bits, together a number between 0000 0000 and FFFF FFFF. The entire program structure is so easy to understand, that after some practice you might actually control it automatically without any paperwork.

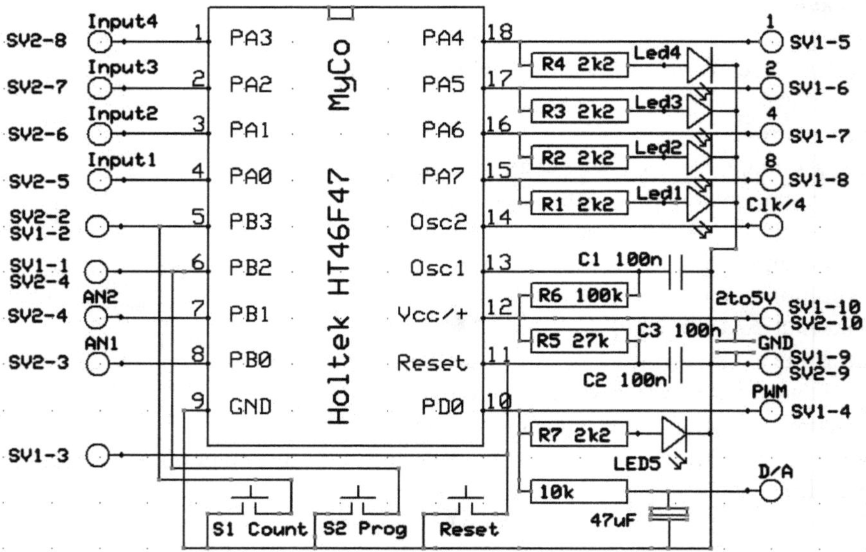

Figure 1.1: Circuit diagram including SV1 and SV2 connections

To make it easy for the reader, and for people who would like to do more with it, I suggest and use a free software package from Expresspcb at
http://www.expresspcb.com
and you can draw your own schematics.

It is simple to learn and covers both aspects: to draw the schematics and to do a PCB design. When you are ready, you can even send your own design to them to have your PCB made.

Figure 1.1 shows a slightly simplified PCB of the system with all of the components included, that are always needed. On the board there is a provision for 2 additional connectors for external interfacing – SV1 and SV2.

Figure 1.2 shows the complete circuit diagram. For easy understanding some parts are left out, but I added the RC for the DA converter, though it is not on the PCB – but for me part of the unit.

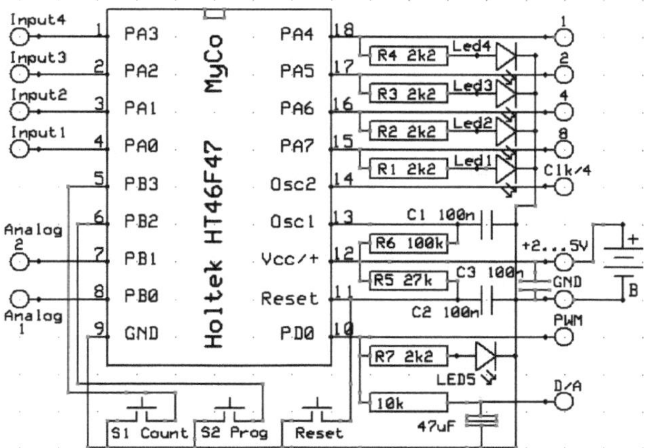

Figure 1.2: Circuit diagram of the board, reduced to main functions

Most external connections are accessible in multiple ways. The large solder terminals are suitable for simple experiments with directly soldered-on components or via soldering on wires. Screw terminals can be used as well, but another option is to solder on flexible wires to the terminals and have the screw terminals at the end of these wires, where you need them. In addition, the option of the 2 ten pin headers is provided, allowing for connection via ribbon cables. These are not supplied with the learning kit and may be added later if necessary.

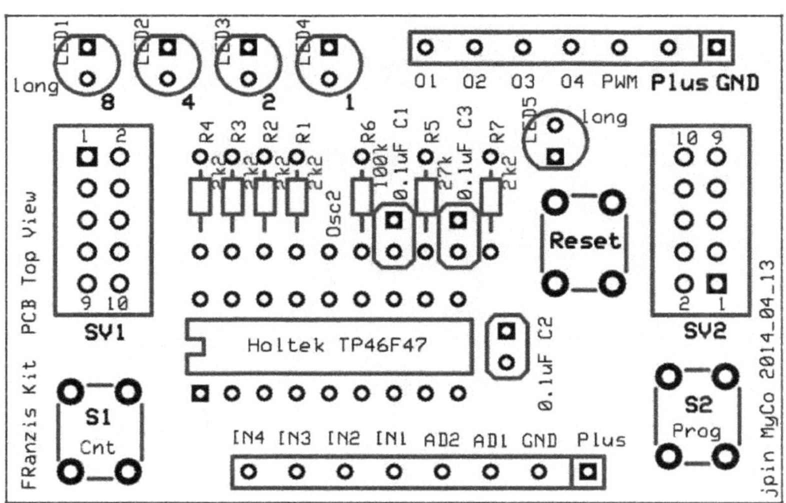

Figure 1.3: Component locations top view of the board, about 40 x 60 mm

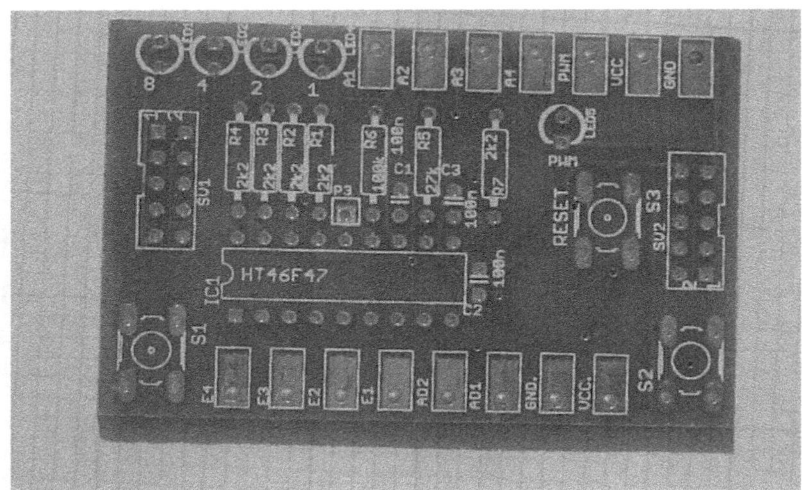

Figure 1.4t: The blank PCB, with the 4 Output LEDs 8,4,2,1 top left

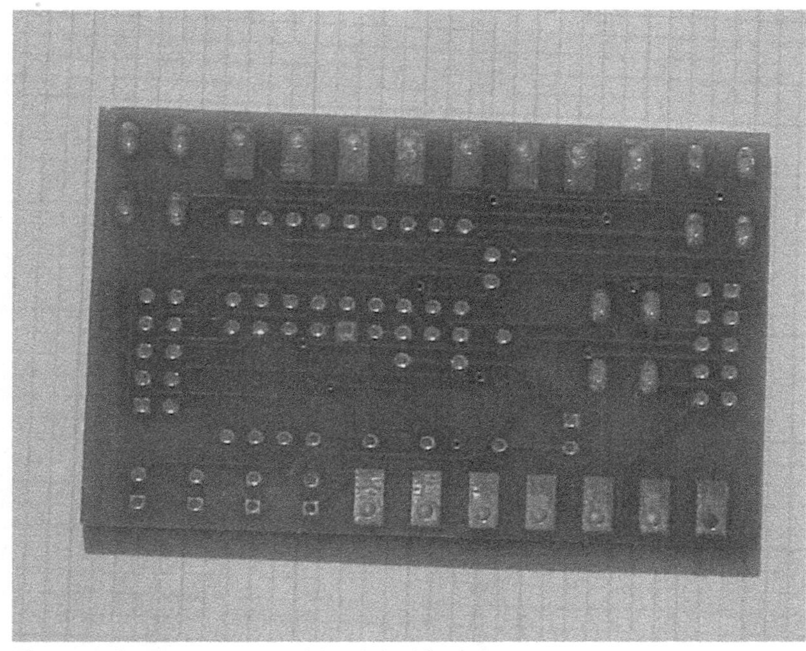

Figure 1.4bottom: Bottom side of the blank PCB

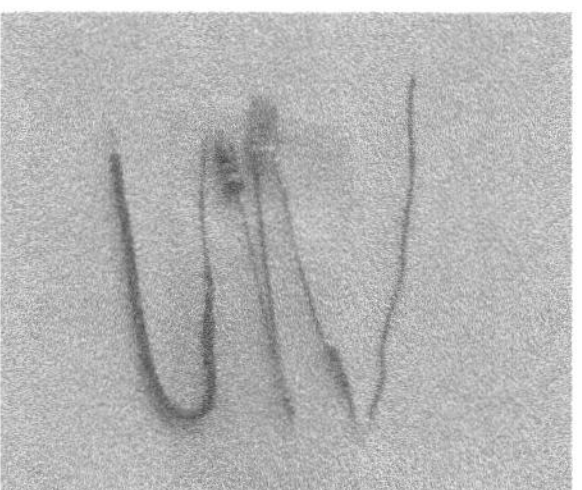

Figure 1.4led: Additional possible LED tester using the PWM resistor and LED

The board is labeled with all of the component values, so assembly should not be a problem. The microcontroller is added via the IC socket later, so the board can be pre-tested before you insert it. As well the chip can be programmed in this socket, then removed and incorporated into other circuits. Pay attention to the correct direction of the four red LEDs, whose cathodes (short wire) have to be inserted to the PCB edge side (square solder pad). Leave all external ports and connectors initially unconnected.

And - do not solder in R7 and LED5 yet, as we can use them as board tester before the IC is inserted, see Figure 1.4l. For now, just solder the resistor to the long end of the PWM LED, add a bit of bare wire at the end of the LED, and a bit with the red still on to the resistor; insulate the area where the bare wires are with some transparent tape on top and bottom, so the LED cannot be destroyed unintentionally.

Solder on the red and black wire of the battery compartment to the PCB and insert the 3 cells, the correct direction is shown on the bottom of the battery compartment. The first test is now for the battery: connect the two open ends of your tester to VCC and GND top right, and if the LED lights up, this part is ok.

If you are confident that you built it all correctly, remove at least one cell to switch power off and then insert the IC carefully, notch to the left. You might have to bend one side of the leads a little bit so it fits. Now check visually, that all pins are in the socket, one got bent in mine. If you are not sure if you soldered all of the parts correctly, you can check with your tester before you insert the IC and see roughly, if the voltage levels are correct.

For later: Note, that the PWM LED cathode has a different mounting direction than the remaining four LEDs, short wire direction of this PWM LED (cathode) to the middle of the board. If all has been tested ok, add PWM LED and R now: remove the insulation, unsolder resistor and LED and insert and solder them in carefully. Now insert the IC and put the cells back in to switch your MyCo on; LED 1 and 8 should blink now.

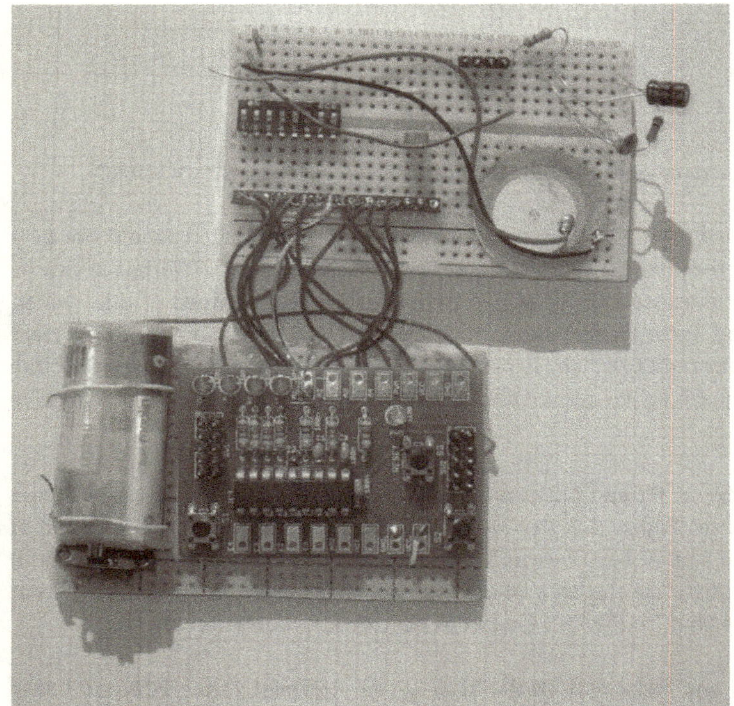

Figure 1.5: Standard setup with push-button switches and my added extension board

Figure 1.6: The use of screw terminals on top side

Figure 1.6 shows the possible placement of screw terminals. If you want to use these connections with screw terminals later, take into account that you should not solder anything onto the pads before, as otherwise you might not be able to mount them easily. While it may be possible to remove the excess lead from the holes later, it still means more work and the danger that copper might come off the PCB.

For a possible connection of external components such as power drivers, relay drivers or opt couplers, you can use the pin headers. I suggest straight type on the left and angled on the right to have better access to S1 and S2 as shown in Figure 1.7.

Figure 1.7: Use of the two pin header connectors

All of the solder connections are also accessible via the pin headers. The outputs are available on SV1 on the left, SV2 on the right has the inputs. On both connectors there is access to the supply voltage, so you can supply the board either via the ribbon cable or you can also power external peripherals from the device connected to the system power supply. On SV1 there is as well reset, S1 and S2, so all connections are provided, ready to program the system from the outside.

S2	1	2	**S1**
Reset	3	4	**PWM**
A1	5	6	**A2**
A3	7	8	**A4**
GND	9	10	**VCC**

Header connector SV1, as on the board

VCC	10	9	**GND**
E4	8	7	**E3**
E2	6	5	**E1**
AD2	4	3	**AD1**
S1	2	1	**S2**

Header connector SV2, (as on the board, turned 180°)

2 - Hardware Tests

Some basic programs are already loaded into the MyCo controller IC (default) and they can be started immediately. You get to know MyCo step by step, before starting to program yourself. Familiarize yourself with the hardware and software features first, before you start with your own programming.
For our first tests we will use the small programs that are already in the controller. You can find all for the program listings in the Appendix. Detailed explanations of all instructions used will follow a bit later in chapter 3.

2.1 - The Basic Structure

Now we can really start. Connect the power supply again, or you might have left it on anyway. Ensure again the correct polarity of the battery cells with the negative (black) to GND and the positive (red) to VCC.

The Holtek microcontroller HT46F47 is clocked by its internal RC oscillator. The external resistor and capacitor at the Osc1 input determine the clock frequency. With 100 kOhm and 100nF, a frequency of approximately 2 MHz is set.

If required, the programs can be running with a lower or higher speed by changing them. For faster execution solder a resistor of 33k in parallel to the 100k for a speed of about 4x. Capacitor C3 between VCC and GND is used for the smoothing of the supply voltage only and has no effect on clock frequency. The Osc2 output remains unused in this booklet. If necessary, you can connect an additional resistor to VCC and get pulses with a quarter of the clock frequency. One idea might be to add a CD4060 or a similar counter onto the breadboard and have many different subdivided frequencies available at the different outputs of this chip for your own projects.

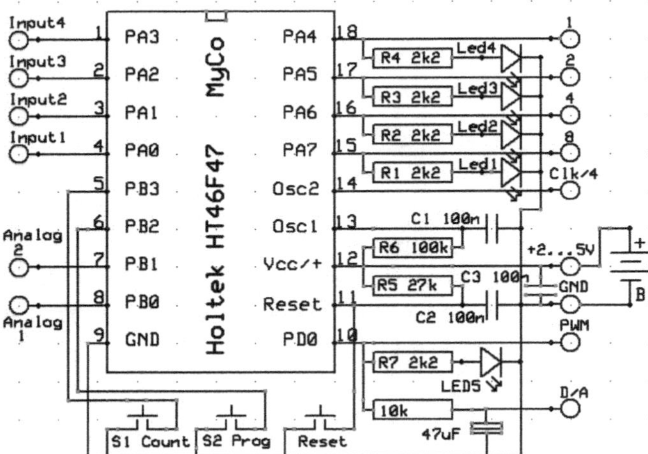

Figure 2.1: Four LEDs on the outputs

This covers most of the components on the board except for the low pass 10k resistor and 47uF capacitor in the schematic at the output of the Pulse Width Modulation signal to generate a quasi-analog signal, but I added them to the schematic anyway so it is not forgotten about, and for me it is part of the unit.

There is no power switch as part of this system. For switching off, just take one of the cells out of the compartment. Once you have soldered on the battery compartment, the two wires should always remain connected if possible, otherwise you might damage the solder connections due to excessive heating. The alternative is to get a little sliding switch, cut the red wire and solder in the switch in an appropriate position.

As you can see I put a larger PCB underneath the controller board to protect against short circuits at the bottom, and mounted a battery and switch http://www.maplin.co.uk/p/single-pole-sub-miniature-ff77j on there as well. Or ask on ebay. A nice little unit which just fits into a small case I found at Maplin. Take the connector out of the breadboard I found there as well and the breadboard fits into another little case of the same type. Rubber band around both, and all is nicely protected. As batteries you can use either the 3 AA that fit the case supplied, or the 2x AAA I use, other options are rechargeable NMH batteries or one protected rechargeable Lithium cell.

2.2 - Two flashing LEDs

When you connect power, the first program starts automatically as we have seen before, an alternating flasher with LED8 and LED1, at a frequency of about 1 Hz. Program listing 2.1 shows how simple this program is, only five lines of code. LED1 and LED8 are turned on alternatively.

Address	Instruction	Data	Comment
20	1	1	LED 1 on, out 0001
21	2	8	Wait for 500 ms
22	1	8	LED 8 on, out 1000
23	2	8	Wait for 500 ms
24	3	4	Jump to - 4

Listing 2.1: Switch on one LED and then another one

After power on, the processor looks at the input lines and sees they are all high, as of the internal pull-up resistors in the chip. As result a jump to address 20 where the program starts:

at 20 Instruction 1 means, send this data to the output and as well to the LEDs
The value 1 in hex means 0001 in binary, so the lowest LED,
LED 1 is switched on

at 21 Instruction 2 tells the processor to execute a waiting loop
Value 8 defines the length as 8 units = 500ms,
see Instruction Table

at 22 Instruction 1 we had before, send the data value to output
Value 8 in hex defines 1000 in binary, so only LED8
switched on

at 23 Instruction 2 tells the processor to execute a waiting loop
Value 8 defines the length as 8 = 500ms,
see Instruction Table

at 24 Instruction 3 defines a jump back from the current location
Value 4 defines how far back, with 4 it means jump back
from 24 to 20

We are now in an infinite loop, executing the same instructions all over.

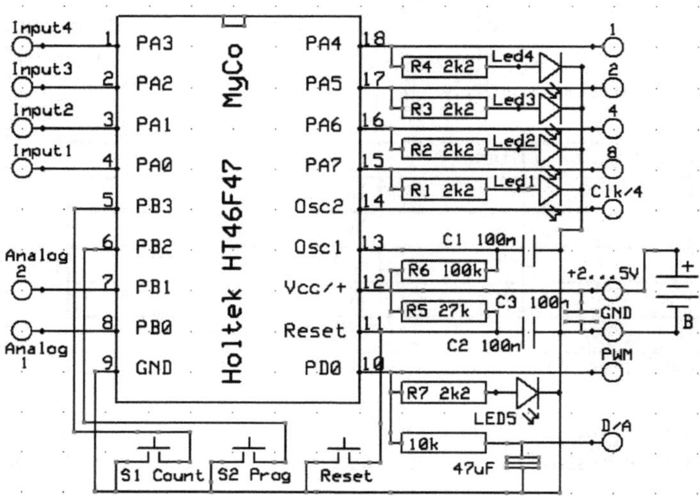

Figure 2.2: No extra wiring for this program listing 2.1

If the LEDs do not blink as expected, you can double check by measuring the voltages at different pins of the IO, the reset switch, and the oscillator pin, as you might have done using our LED tester:

VCC:	4.5 V for 3 AA, 3V for 2 AAA
Reset:	4.5V for 3 AA, 3V for 2 AAA
Osc1:	1.5 V
E1 to E4:	4.5 V (but not with our LED tester)
A1:	changing between 0 and 4.5V
A2, A3: 0V	
A3:	changing between 0 and 4.5V if you use 3 cells

2.3 - Counter combined with PWM

Now let's see how a counter works. To tell the processor which one of the stored progams to execute, we connect IN1 to ground. The simplest way is to push a short wire into the E1 and GND holes and remove the wire again after trying the program. I have chosen to put a bit more flexibility in and prepare for further programming. All of the major MyCo connections are on my added interface that plugs into the breadboard, including all of the inputs and outputs and GND.

See as well the appendix. The relevant DIL switch is now changed from open to closed and on the other side connected to GND and we switch on power again.
All of the digital inputs are normally pulled high via a resistor inside the controller chip to VCC (pull-up resistor). The wire or switch changes this input signal now to low and the processor recognises this when starting the program. Look at the PWM output to see how it gets brighter in 16 steps as the LEDs show the counting up.

MyCo Function Symbol

IN1 to GND

IN4	PA3	PA4	01
IN3	PA2	PA5	02
IN2	PA1	PA6	04
IN1	PA0	PA7	08
S1	PB3	Osc2	
S2	PB2	Osc1	
AD2	PB1	Vcc/+	+
AD1	PB0	Reset	RES
GND	GND	PD0	PWM

Figure 2.3: Counter and PWM function shown via the LED

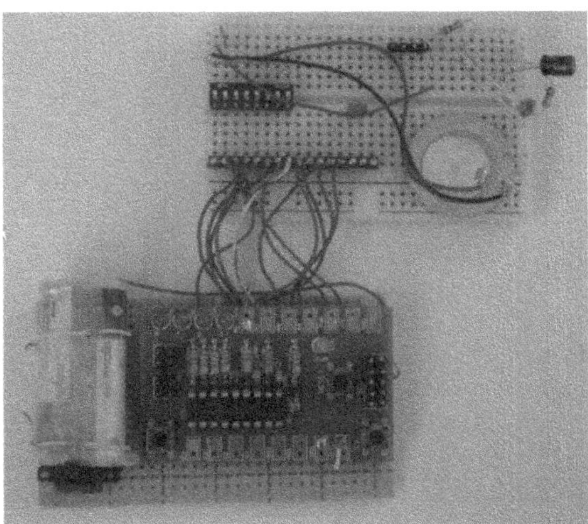

Figure 2.4: The binary counter

Pulling down the IN1 line is actually only required for the start of the program, when the controller checks via the inputs what to do, if you use the pre-programmed code. So, for this experiment, only temporarily hold a wire to the terminals while you switch on power. With IN1 low after a reset, the second example program starts, located at address 25. As a quick look at the code comment states:

A+1 is added to the accumulator A, then the contents of A is sent to the 4 LEDs and then to the PWM generator. There is a delay of 0.1 secs and a jump back to the beginning.
The PWM generator basically changes the 16 steps 0 to 15, that you can see on the 4 LEDs, into 16 time slots of a set frequency.

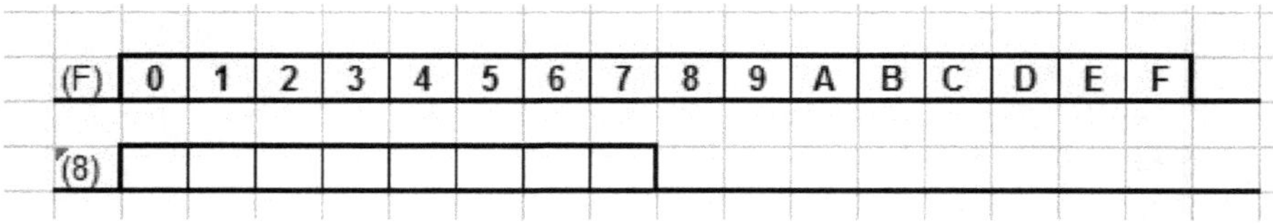

(F)	0	1	2	3	4	5	6	7	8	9	A	B	C	D	E	F
(8)																

At the beginning, no slot on, so signal 0, PWM LED dark; then 1 slot used, 15 off, rather dim. In the end the PWM LED is completely on showing the value 15. Then the loop starts again with 0 = off

Address	Instruction	Data	Comment
25	7	1	A <= A + 1
26	5	4	Port <= A
27	5	9	PWM <= A
28	2	6	Wait 100 ms
29	3	4	Jump to - 4

Listing 2.2: Binary counter with LED and PWM output

The LEDs show all combinations of binary numbers from 0000 to FFFF. The LED numbers 1, 2, 4, 8 show the weight they have so as you go through the 16 possibilities, add the binary weights and you have the decimal weight 0 to 15. As 10 to 15 would need 2 digits to describe the status, it would make the reading of a longer string of numbers rather difficult, so 10 to 15 have been replaced by A, B, C, D, E and F, and we have 1 digit for 0 to 15. Problem solved the secret behind hexadecimal numbers revealed. Just to throw some more knowledge in: these 4 bits are called a nibble.

In all of our code we have an instruction nibble and a data nibble; the 2 nibbles combined to 8 bits we call a byte. So at all addresses 8 bits are stored, we use an 8 bit processor. For comparison, in a PC the processor is 32 or 64 bit wide, equal to 4 or 8 bytes.

„8“	„4“	„2“	„1“	Decimal	Hexadecimal
0	0	0	0	0	0
0	0	0	1	1	1
0	0	1	0	2	2
0	0	1	1	3	3
0	1	0	0	4	4
0	1	0	1	5	5
0	1	1	0	6	6
0	1	1	1	7	7
1	0	0	0	8	8
1	0	0	1	9	9
1	0	1	0	10	A
1	0	1	1	11	B
1	1	0	0	12	C
1	1	0	1	13	D
1	1	1	0	14	E
1	1	1	1	15	F

4 Bit in binary, decimal and hexadecimal

If you look at this program output in a different way, it actually outputs 4 different frequencies on the 4 output lines O1, O2, O4, O8. Starting at the lowest bit, the next higher one is frequency divided by 2 or pulse length is times 2. Please do not be confused as the delay loop is only 100ms. For each complete signal it must be 100ms on and 100ms off = 200ms (so 2 times through this program).

A1: 200 ms	**= 5**	**Hz**
A2: 400 ms	**= 2.5**	**Hz**
A3: 800 ms	**= 1.25**	**Hz**
A4: 1600 ms	**= 0.625**	**Hz**

The output signal of the PWM output shows a different behavior. The PWM signal is a square wave, where the on and off time changes with a fixed repetition frequency of approximately 16kHz. The pulse length of high and low is controlled by the data value, and the pulse / pause ratio determines the average duty cycle and so the brightness of the LED. The brightness of the PWM LED is controlled in 16 steps between 0 and 15 for full brightness.

This digital PWM output signal can be converted into a quasi-DC voltage via the low pass filter of 10 k and 47 uF, see circuit diagram Figure 1.2. The PWM output after the filter is thus an analog signal. With this program, you will output a gradually rising voltage from 0 V to 4.5V DC. Follow the voltage profile with a meter or an oscilloscope. You might later reprogram this code by changing it from the 100ms to a longer delay to see the ramp more clearly on your analog meter. With a digital meter it might otherwise even be more difficult to see the changing DC voltage.

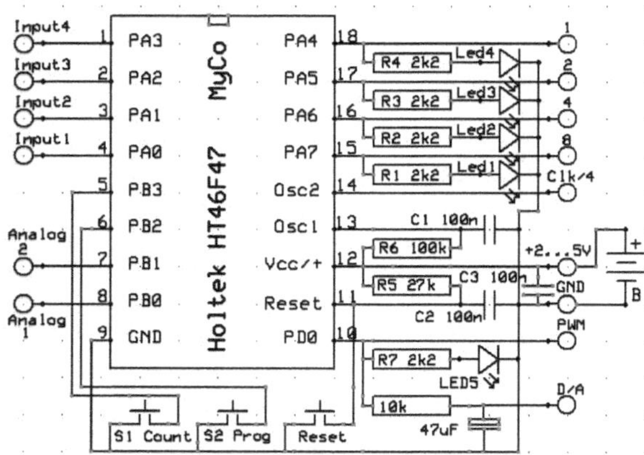

Figure 2.5: Low-pass filter on the PWM output

Figure 2.6: Smoothened PWM output voltage as analog output

You can build this low pass as well by direct connection on the controller board. A resistor of 10k from the PWM hole to AD2 hole which is free and not used in this experiment, and is as well then the smoothened analog output, and the 47uF capacitor from the same AD2 hole to ground. As before I use my external breadboard. The same setup will be used later in a program, where MyCo checks via the AD2 input if the analog voltage is above or below a predefined value and takes decisions accordingly.

2.4 - The Analog-to-Digital Converter

With a connection of E2 to GND and pressing the reset button, a small example program starts to show the function of the internal A/D block (ADC). The analog voltage on input AD1 is measured and converted into a digital numerical value. As MyCo always operates with 4 bit values, the result of an analog-to-digital conversion is a number in the range 0 to 15. The result is 0, if the input voltage is 0, the result 15 to a voltage which corresponds to about the operating voltage, which is for example, 4.0 V. The AD value is output as a binary number to the four LEDs and additionally sent to the PWM output. For this experiment we use the Light Dependent Resistor (LDR) to ground and AD1, and a resistor of 10kOhm from AD1 to Plus, building a voltage divider.

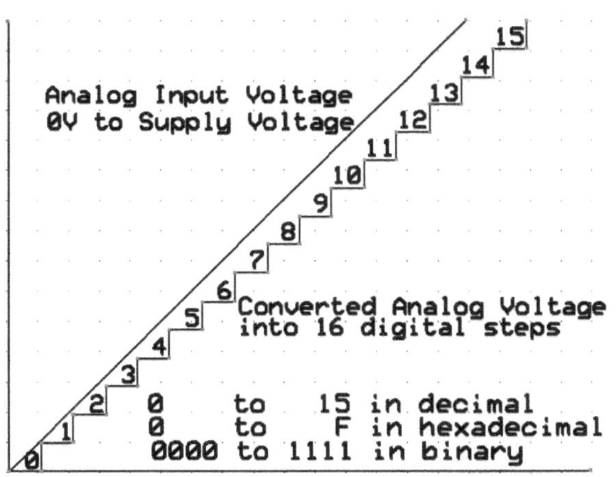

A table of the input voltage and the expected LED display if supply voltage is 4.0V:

Step	0	1	2	3	4	5	6	7
Volt	0.00	0.25	0.50	0.75	1.00	1.25	1.50	1.75

Step	8	9	A	B	C	D	E	F
Volt	2.00	2.25	2.50	2.75	3.00	3.25	3.50	3.75

Measure the actual voltage at the input with a high impedance input voltmeter to compare. Other resistors than 10k would give a different response to a given range of light.

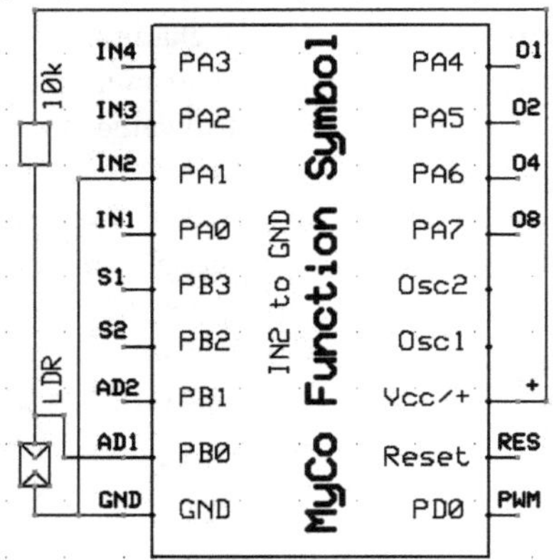

Figure 2.7: Connection of the light sensor

Figure 2.8: The LDR connected to input of AD1

The example program is easy to understand, as it is basically the same as the counter and PWM program. The only difference is the source of the data to output to LEDs and PWM - before it was from the counter, now from the A/D converter.

The resolution is limited to 4 bit, 16 switching steps as in the table. You can experiment with a slightly changed setup, and have a resistor in series with the 10k, and an additional resistor between LDR and ground, or a resistor in parallel with the LDR to see different ranges.
And there are other sensors that you can try in your own experiments.

Address	Instruction	Data	Comment
2A	6	9	A <= AD1
2B	5	4	Port <= A
2C	5	9	PWM <= A
2D	2	6	Wait 100 ms
2E	3	4	Jump to - 4

Listing 2.3: AD converter and PWM output

Test the program using different light sources for the sensor. The more light falls on to the LDR, the smaller the resistance of the LDR and as consequence the voltage to AD1 goes down. On the other end, you will achieve maximum AD values on the 4 LEDs in the dark, giving you maximum brightness on the PWM output in the dark.
Make a table of different light conditions and try to repeat them.
Swap LDR and resistor and see what happens.

2.5 - Random Number Generator

With a jumper wire from E3 to GND you will play with a very basic Random Number Generator. Remember, the MyCo symbol in figure 2.9 covers the whole board including switches and LEDs. You can see what has to be added externally to the board.

You will normally not be able to predict the result on the LEDs for such a random number generator, but as we only have a range of 16 possibilities with our 4 bit computer, luck might strike. In this example the status of S1 is tested. See the instruction at address 31, listing 2.4. As with all other inputs the internal pull-up resistor keeps the input value at High, until the button is pressed and changes the input voltage to zero.

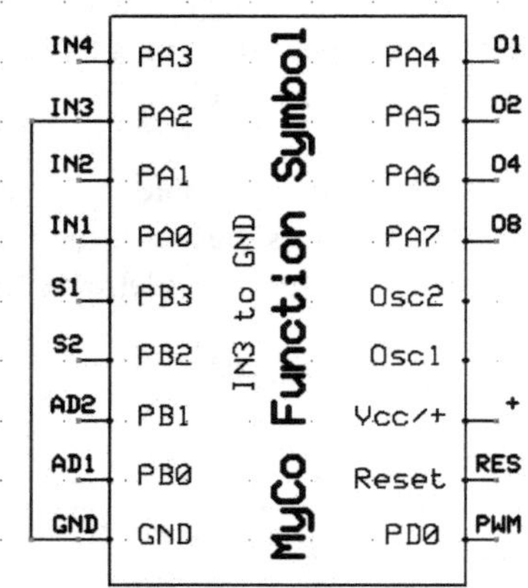

Figure 2.9: Start of the random number generator

Figure 2.10: Wire bridge between E3 and GND

This program uses a new instruction that we need for decisions. There are different names for this and different people have different opinions. Some would call it a conditional branch instruction. But then I would expect that I can branch to a number of locations, similar to the Jump instruction that you could call an unconditional branch to a range of possible addresses.

This for me is a Skip Instruction. In the Instruction Table you find a clear definition:

CE = Skip if S1 = 1

So, what happens in these 4 lines of the program?

The contents of the Accumulator A is sent to the 4 LEDs 1 2 4 8.

Then the program tests if the S1 input state is High, so the button is not pushed yet. Then the following instruction is skipped over and we stay in the same loop until the button is pushed, a loop waiting for action. When pushed, S1 is NOT 1 anymore, the increment instruction is not skipped anymore.

Now Accumulator A is incremented, and the program stays in this fast increment loop and outputs values to the LEDs, as long as the button is pushed. When you then release the button, the counter A is not incremented anymore and you are back to the first loop described and the random number is displayed. As this counting up is very fast, you cannot really control it, so the result is random.

Address	Instruction	Data	Comment
30	5	4	Port <= A
31	C	E	S1 = 1?
32	7	1	A<= A + 1
33	3	3	Jump to - 3

Listing 2.4: Random Number Generator

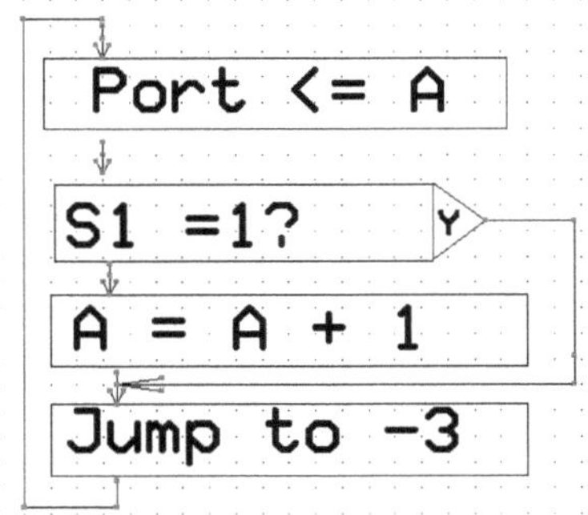

Program flow shown in a different way

Test different results of this experiment, and you should as well document the numbers via a table to show the results. The more results you write in, the better distributed the result should be. After a sufficient number of runs the table should show the same or similar in all numbers from 0 to F.
You can play this as well as a game, where two or more people have a sheet and fill in their results. Who reaches the end of one number first, wins.

0	1	2	3	4	5	6	7	8	9	A	B	C	D	E	F

Learnig Hexadecimal as Game

With this program you can test the operational speed of this system. Per each instruction the execution speed is about 1ms. The final output frequency of LED 8 is about 16Hz, you might see the flicker.
This processor runs at a clock speed of 2MHz by using the 100k resistor. At 4.5 Volt supply voltage you can solder a 33k resistor in parallel to the 100k and execution speed will be about 4x, but check on the data sheet at which supply voltages such a speed is allowed. See the link in the appendix.

2.6 - Pulse Length Measurement

With E4 connected to GND, you start a program that measures the time between releasing the Reset and push S1.

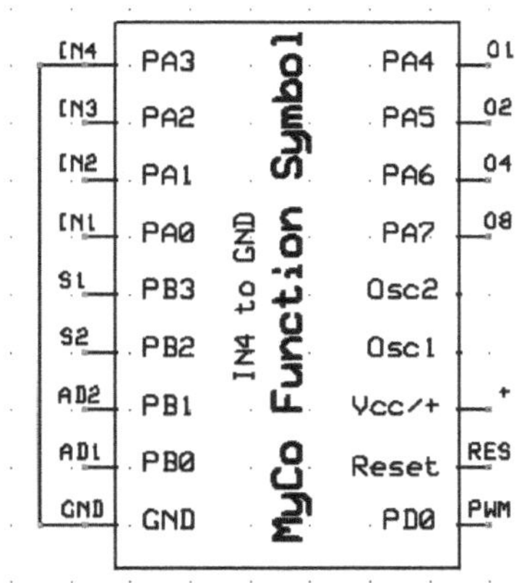

Figure 2.11: E4 to GND

Figure 2.12: Pulse length measurement using Reset and S1

The first 3 addresses are a delay, 1 instruction to test if S1 is Low, so pushed and a jump back if not. If yes, then go to address 37 to set A to 0, wait for 5 ms, increment A, send the A contents to the LEDs, and check if S1 has been released =1, if not, restart the increment loop again, else go to address 3D, jump back to the beginning and restart at address 34. You have the waiting time set to 5ms at address 38; each instruction takes 1ms, so the sum time is 10ms. This means that the pulse length resolution of this measurement is 10ms.

Address	Instruction	Data	Comment
34	2	2	Wait for 5 ms
35	C	C	S1 = 0?
36	3	2	Jump to - 2
37	4	0	A <= 0
38	2	2	Wait for 5 ms
39	7	1	A <= A + 1
3A	5	4	Port <= A
3B	C	E	S1 = 1?
3C	3	4	Jump to - 4
3D	3	9	Jump to - 9

Listing 2.5: Time measurement

Press the S1 key for as short a time as possible after letting Reset go and the program counts the length. You get, for example, the result of 1010, i.e. decimal 10. Since the time unit of the program is 10ms, the displayed time is 100ms. With some training you will probably be able to come down to reach even shorter times, probably down to 50ms, or in other words a pulse length of 20th sec.

3 - The Programming Mode

Until now we have only used programs that had been stored in there as delivered. The fun starts, when you begin modifying them. For example, you could just change the Wait time from 5ms to 50ms, modify code 22 to 25 in listing 2.5 at address 38. And do not worry about making mistakes; if you did something wrong, and nothing works anymore, then just "push the software reset button" and get all of the pre-programmed code back - as delivered. We will show you soon how to do it.

It is difficult to believe it, but to write programs/change in this device, you only need the 3 switches, even to enter the numbers. I must complement Burkhard for this genius idea. Basically, you need S1 (left) for data entry, and S2 (right hand side) for programming. The Reset button is used as well to start the programming cycle. Only these 3 switches are required to step through the program, change it, program the new value into the chip, and start the new program. And there are only very few instructions that this device executes, they will be explained very soon.

3.1 - First - Reading out Programs

Switch on power, and the 2 LEDs start blinking as before. A good test showing it all works well, like a small self-test of the system. You can now enter into the Programming Mode by holding down S2 and then Reset. Release the Reset switch first, but keep S2 down for at least half a second, the minimum time for the Interpreter program in the IC to recognize that you want to enter the Programming Mode.

LED 4 and 2 light up and show 6, this is the pre-programmed instruction at address 00. You can now scroll through the program by just using the S2 key to check instructions and data. Each address in the program requires two key operations of S2: you switch between the display of an instruction and then the display of data. In addition, the current address is displayed for short time. Reading it all, needs some practice.

Look in the appendix to find which code is pre-programmed starting from address 00:

64 51 4E 80 C3 98 ...

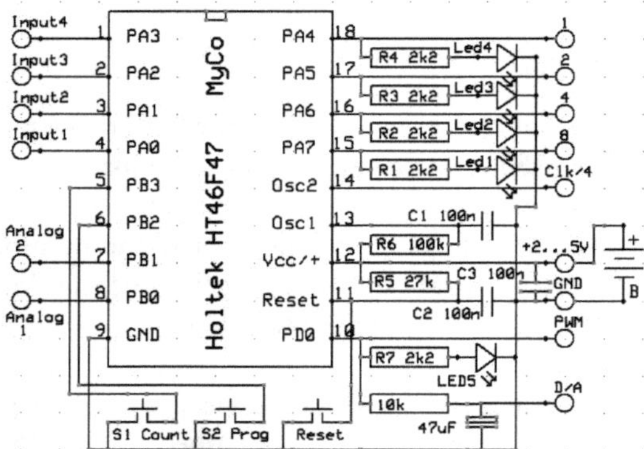

Figure 3.1: S1 and S2 and Reset for the programming mode

Figure 3.2: The three buttons, and the 4 LEDs top left are used

At address 00, instruction 6 is shown (upper nibble)

- First Press of S2
    - Show data (lower nibble)

- Second press of S2
    - Show next address for 300 ms
    - Then show instruction (high nibble)
- Third press of S2
    - Show data (lower nibble)

- And the same block of activity again

Let us first read out a program that is already stored, but for now not change it. You only need to push S2 ten times to do it. As the actual address is shown for a short time, it is easy to verify what happens. You always know, if you are looking at an instruction or at data. As you have not changed the program yet, the originally pre-programmed code is still in there. Let us look at the first five instructions:

Address	Instruction	Data	Comment
00	6	4	A <= Din
01	5	1	B <= A
02	4	E	A <= 14
03	8	0	AddrHi <= 0
04	C	3	A = B?

Listing 3.1: Program code in pre-programmed controller

As you know by now, this whole project is based on 4 bit units, which are called nibbles. Two nibbles are combined into an 8 bit wide byte.
The processor used here has 3 different areas to store information. Some RAM as scratch pad, and the contents in this part will be forgotten when power is switched off. Then the so called Interpreter which is stored permanently in the Flash area, 2k bytes long. Flash is a type of memory that can be overwritten a couple of thousand times and the data stays there when switched off.

Within this area there is a second block of Flash containing a safety copy of the pre-programmed code. The third type is the pre-programmed EEPROM area for your programs, and this is 128 bytes long. Yes, you are reading correctly 1 2 8 b y t e s. Not very much you might think, as your phone and the camera you have contain a lot more memory.

Just to put it into perspective:

128 Byte EEPROM in MyCo as the program area for you
128 Kilobyte would be 1000 times this
128 Megabyte is 1000 x 1000 times more again.
128 Gigabyte is 1000 x 1000 x 1000 times what we use here.
(USB sticks now have mostly 4 to 128GB)

But 128 bytes of program area is enough for many little applications as you will find out.
And do not forget, you do not program the processor directly, but the EEPROM, which tells the Interpreter what to do, so programs are actually a lot more compact.

A bit of digression here and from my own experience: The same technique of a few switches and an Interpreter was used in one of the first video games based on the CDP1802 microprocessor. Joseph Weissbecker developed Chip8 in the 1970s, see more under http://en.wikipedia.org/wiki/CHIP-8.

And here the programming was done in a similar way to save program space as it was expensive then. But you needed 11 switches: 8 to define the 2 nibbles and 3 for control, and 8 LEDs for display, plus an extra one similar to our PWM, but the same principle. I was really impressed to find out, that 3 switches and 4 LEDs still make it possible to write and run programs. Now I am just waiting for someone to do the next implementation of MyCo, which will have a lot more programming area.

Just for fun, you can still beat this minimum interface: with 2 switches, one to input data and one for reset if needed. How would it work? Nothing new really: you will play with it a little bit later - it is called Morse code. You could basically adapt the Interpreter to understand Morse code. As we only use numbers, only a small part of the full code is needed. For more, see Wikipedia http://upload.wikimedia.org/wikipedia/commons/b/b5/International_Morse_Code.svg

Morse Code

A	- ---	J	- --- --- ---	S	- - -	1	- --- --- --- ---
B	--- - - -	K	--- - ---	T	---	2	- - --- --- ---
C	--- - --- -	L	- --- - -	U	- - ---	3	- - - --- ---
D	--- - -	M	--- ---	V	- - - ---	4	- - - - ---
E	-	N	--- -	W	- --- ---	5	- - - - -
F	- - --- -	O	--- --- ---	X	--- - - ---	6	--- - - - -
G	--- --- -	P	- --- --- -	Y	--- - --- ---	7	--- --- - - -
H	- - - -	Q	--- --- - ---	Z	--- --- - -	8	--- --- --- - -
I	- -	R	- --- -			9	--- --- --- --- -
						0	--- --- --- --- ---

But we digressed, let us go back to MyCo again, and its minimum hardware and interface and programming.

3.2 - Programming new Functions

Now it is time to change from exploring how the pre-programmed MyCo works, to changing, writing and programming in other code using S1, S2 and Reset.

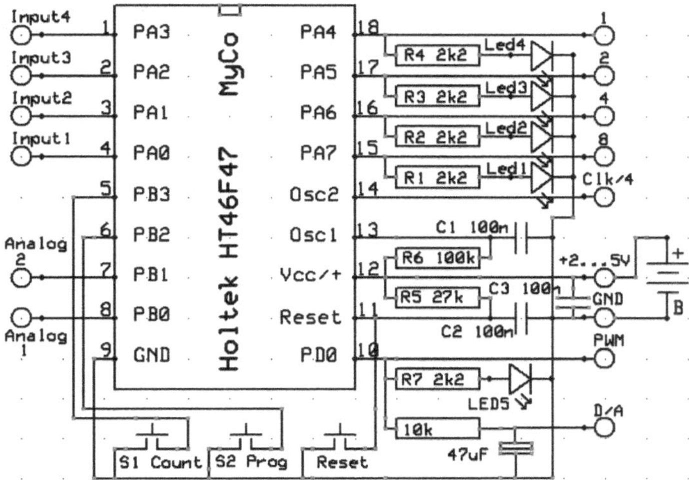

Reading a program, as we just did, and changing the instruction and data at this address location is done in the same programming mode, but now we use S1 in addition to just S2. The function of S1 is to generate a hexadecimal number, that will then be programmed into the Instruction or Data nibble. By pushing S1 you modify / increment an internal counter to get to the right number. If you went too far, no problem, just continue until you reached the correct number is displayed to be programmed in.

The first pressing of S1 resets the internal counter from the original number, so you always start with a clean zero. The status of this internal counter is shown via the 4 LEDs. To get for example to a 4 for programming (either for Instruction or for Data depends on what status you are in), push S1 once to reset counter from the number it contained to zero, the next press increases to 1, then to 2, then to 3, then to 4 – and the S1 job is done.

Activating now S2 will program this nibble which is displayed via the 4 LEDs into the EEPROM. And to show you that programming is hard work (it really does not take that long), there is a 600ms delay when you push S2 for programming. Mentally it is like you handing over the work to a programmer.

After these 600ms the display shows quickly the next address to work on and then changes to the instruction at this location. You do not have to program all nibbles, you can as well step through the addresses and for example just change the length of a delay loop, and the rest stays as is. In Programming Mode, via S2, go to the right address, you can then verify the instruction there and the next nibble will be the Data to be changed.

As a first test enter a very short program, just two instructions. The first instruction turns on LED1, LED2 and LED4, then jumps back to the same location 01 via 30, over and over until you take one of the cells out to switch off the power.

Address	Instruction	Data	Comment
00	1	7	A1...4 <= 0111
01	3	0	Jump to - 0

Listing 3.2: Turn on 3 LEDs

Address	Instruction	Data	Comment
00	6	4	A <= Din
01	5	4	Dout <= A
02	3	2	Jump to -2

Listing 3.2a: Status of IN1, IN2, IN3, IN4 the 4 LEDs

Now let us program a different code with 3 instructions to add input control. We take the status of the 4 input lines into A, send this status to the LEDs and jump back to the beginning. The LEDs should all be on after the first instruction, the internal pull-up resistors in the chip set these lines to High even with nothing connected. With a short wire you can now pull lines low and the relevant LED will switch off. In my little experiment area I prepared for this already, just use DIL switch 1, 2, 3, or 4, no wires needed, and you can see how the LEDs change.

A program listing is a very helpful way for documentation and for understanding what happens. But there is a shorter way of writing down programs: just as a sequence of hex numbers, so the first program would be 17 30, the second one 64 54 31. We do not need to add the hex sign h after the number, as we know we only work with hexadecimal numbers. And we do not need a start address either, as the code blocks in MyCo are mostly not address dependent.

To show the complete sequence to program listing 3.2 into the chip, the following must be done:

S2 + Reset	to put into Programming Mode
2 x S1	to reset counter and increase to 1
S2	program in this 1 and switch to the second nibble
8 x S1	reset counter to 0, then 7x to get to 7
S2	program this 7 in, increment to address 01
4 x S1	reset counter for instruction, 3x to get to 3
S2	program 3 in and change to data
1 x S1	only 1x S1 to reset internal counter
S2	program 0 in

All done, now push Reset shortly, and the 3 LEDs light up.

Note: As we have entered this new program, we have overwritten what was there before, and the blinking 2 LEDs will not start anymore after reset.

Option 1: you overwrite your own program by putting back what was there before: 64 51 4E, see listing in the appendix, address 00, 01, 02. As a quick check, program it in, reset, all back to normal?
This is no problem if you only have to re-program 2 or 3 bytes, but what if there was a lot more? Just read on to 3.3 to find the solution.

3.3 - Back to Factory Status

If you want to go back to the EEPROM status when you switched MyCo on for the first time and had not done any programming yet, there is a simple way prepared for you. The same code that was programmed into the EEPROM, is as well held in the FLASH memory area that you do not have access to - as part of the Interpreter.

After reset, this Interpreter checks always for the first 2 bytes in EEPROM. If it finds at address 00 FF and at address 01 FF, this basically means to the Interpreter Failed, Failed, re-program please. The Interpreter copies these 128 bytes it holds in FLASH memory into the EEPROM area and starts as normal, 2 LEDs blink again. There was a longer delay to start up than normally now, because the programming of the EEPROM takes a little bit of time.

Address	Instruction	Data	Comment
00	F	F	-
01	F	F	-

Listing 3.3: Return controller to the pre-programmed state

To check, program in example listing 3.2a again and test it by pulling down the relevant input E1 ... E4 (or use the relevant positions of the DIL switch in the breadboard you might have by now). Now reprogram the first 2 locations with FF FF and reset. The LEDs start blinking again. Back to factory set-up.

4 - MyCo Instructions

As we know now how to check and program the code in, it is time to understand which Instructions are actually available to tell this controller what to do.
The Interpreter in MyCo understands 14 instructions and then "interprets" these commands by executing the actual machine code that the Holtek microprocessor understands.

4.1 - The Basic Commands MyCo can execute

Until now we have only seen the outside, meaning the PCB, LEDs, switches ...
Now let's see what happens inside this system and it will become clear very quickly what these instructions do.
To ensure there is no misunderstanding: we have to distinguish 2 types of instructions in this controller. The ones we work with, let us call them I-Instructions to make clear that I program them, or this is what the I_nterpreter understands. Each I-Instruction triggers a piece of code in the Interpreter running the actual microprocessor instructions, the machine code. If you want to have a look at the microprocessor instructions, the link to the Holtek data sheet is in the Appendix. We are only concerned with the I-Instructions.

The large block in 4.1 consists of parts we do not have access to, except for the EEPROM. There is the FLASH memory containing the Interpreter, some RAM to store data, a program counter that runs the Interpreter and many other functions not used in this project. There are 2 additional hidden blocks you do not have really have access to, one is the Delay Unit and the other one the Skip Control block. We will come back to this when we discuss the relevant instructions.

The central block is the A Register, it is involved in many instructions as we will see. Data can travel in and out of these blocks. AD1 and AD2 are the analog-to-digital converters which take the analog signals at the input and convert a voltage between 0 and Vcc into 16 steps, a 4 bit nibble. The PWM unit gets a 4 bit word sent and modifies it into a rectangular output signal by changing the on and off time of a 16 slot long timing unit according to the 4 bit value; averaged outside via the RC it generates a quasi-analog output signal.

The ALU (Arithmetic and Logic Unit) has 3 connections as you can see: Reg A sends data directly, this is combined with data from another source via the bus, and the result goes back into Reg A. We will see this more clearly when we discuss the relevant instructions and the data flow. Input and output we know already, each 4 bit wide.

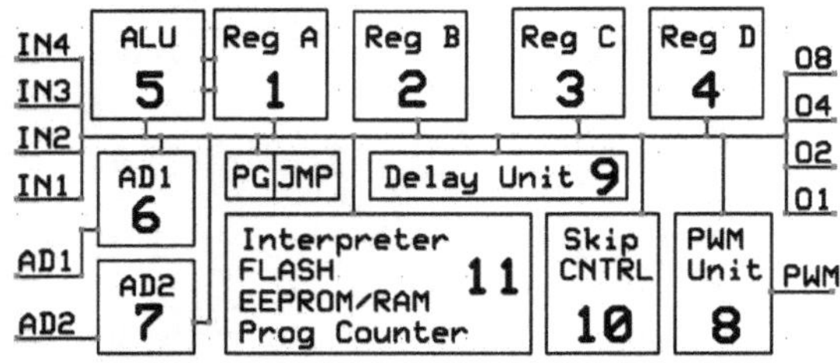

Figure 4.1a: Programming model as block

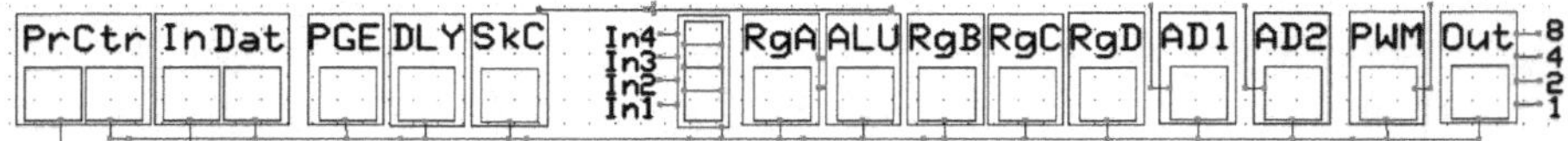

Figure 4.1b: Programming model in string form for program execution on paper

The different blocks in this string:

PrCtr Program counter needs 2 nibbles
In Dat Instruction and Data nibbles
PGE Page register
DLY Delay time
SkC Skip Control bit, if Yes then skip

In_n 4 input lines
RgA Register A
ALU Arithmetic and Logic Unit
RgB Register B
RgC Register C
RgD Register D
AD1 Analog-to-digital converter 1
AD2 Analog-to-digital converter 2
PWM Pulse Width Modulation output
OUT Output register
1248 4 bit output and LEDs

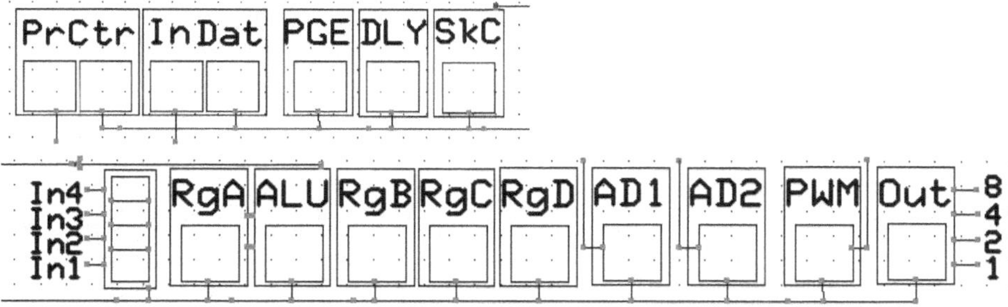

Figure 4.1c: Programming model as 2 blocks for program execution on paper

From now on we will write all instructions as a byte, 2 nibbles of 4 bit; and we know, that the higher part is the Instruction, and the lower nibble is either just a hexadecimal number or the second part of the Instruction. It will become clearer soon.

Let's start with the first 3 Instructions:

10 ... 1F: **Direct Output** of a number to O1...O4,
so the lower nibble actually defines which LED is on,
a value between 0000-1111, in short
this instruction is 1n, where n is the number

20 ... 2F: **Waiting Time** 0...15: (1, 2, 5, 10, 20, 50, 100, 200,
500 ms, 1, 2, 5, 10, 20, 30, 60 s)
So, we can call it as well 2n, as the n defines
a waiting time only

30 ... 3F: **Jump Back** 0...15 lines in the program,
with the current one as starting point 0
You take the address where the instruction is and
count n lines up, so 3n

We have just learnt 48 instructions, as these are 3 instructions and 16 options each:

1 is easy to remember **One**, the first letter gives you the **O** for output
2 is as simple, because wait takes **T(W)OO** long
3 is a bit more difficult, but for now you **THRow** the ball back

And having read these last 3 lines a few times, you will probably never forget these 3 instructions.

You will probably smile now about the following explanation in so many words: Instruction 1 is used to output a constant number to the output port. Thus, any bit pattern can be output and can turn on multiple LEDs simultaneously.

The wait command 2 uses a parameter that contains the time in milliseconds and is defined in steps of 1-2-5 to make it easier for calculations. We can only use our numbers 0 to 15, but this can already achieve delays from 1ms to 60 seconds. Longer delay times are possible when you execute the same delay again or execute a program that counts the amount of delay loops done.

Instruction 3 is particularly simple but is sufficient for many tasks where an operation has to be repeated endlessly. The jump distance is limited to a maximum range of 15. As the jump distance is relative to the current address, program blocks can be moved to other addresses without changing the jump distance number.
The first example program from section 2.2 only needed these three commands. You can see that the start address, there was 20 and is here 00, but the hex code is identical: 11 28 18 28 34.

Address	Instruction	Data	Comment
00	1	1	A1...4 <= 0001
01	2	8	Wait for 500 ms
02	1	8	A1...4 <= 1000
03	2	8	Wait for 500 ms
04	3	4	Jump to - 4

Listing 4.1: Blink program, hex 11 28 18 28 34

With just these 3 Instructions you can already write many little programs. Practice and test the next three programs. The goal should be that you can apply these commands intuitively, and this means practice.

Address	Instruction	Data	Comment
00	1	1	LEDs to 0001
01	2	8	Wait for 500 ms
02	1	2	LEDs to 0010
03	2	8	Wait for 500 ms

04	1	4	LEDs to 0100
05	2	8	Wait for 500 ms
06	1	8	LEDs to 1000
07	2	8	Wait for 500 ms
08	3	8	Jump to - 8

11 28 12 28 14 28 18 28 38

Listing 4.2: Running Light 1

Here the program is extended, so one LED on is lighting up right to left, then left to right, in an endless loop.

Address	Instruction	Data	Comment
00	1	1	LEDs 0001
01	2	8	Wait for 500 ms
02	1	2	LEDs 0010
03	2	8	Wait for 500 ms
04	1	4	LEDs 0100
05	2	8	Wait for 500 ms
06	1	8	LEDs 1000
07	2	8	Wait for 500 ms
08	1	4	LEDs 0100
09	2	8	Wait for 500 ms
0A	1	2	LEDs 0010
0B	2	8	Wait for 500 ms
0C	3	C	Jump to - 12

11 28 12 28 14 28 18 28 14 28 12 28 3C

Listing 4.3: Running Light 2, right to left and back

In an earlier program we measured a pulse length. We can as well do the inverse and generate a pulse length, and there is our tea Timer. When the LEDs switch off, the tea is ready. You can only get out of this program via Reset, running in an infinite loop jumping back to the same location, which serves as the end of program. Extend it to have a three-minute kitchen timer: just execute 2F 3 times in sequence before you do 10 30, or you could send 1111 to the LEDs and wait for 1min, send 0111 and wait for 1min, send 0011 and wait 1min, send 0001 and wait for 1 minute, send 0000 and 4 minutes are over. Many options to train your programming skills.

Address	Instruction	Data	Comment
00	1	F	LEDs to 1111
01	2	F	Wait for 1 min
02	1	0	LEDs to 0000
03	3	0	End

1F 2F 10 30

Listing 4.4: Timer for one minute

4.2 - Calculations using Variables

Until now, only constant values have been used as parameters for individual instructions. This is useful, if a program always executes in the same way. In contrast, complex programs often work with variable data, for example, a calculation such as A = A + B is executed. Depending on the contents of variables A and B, each time the result will be different. This result could then control the LEDs on the outputs.

Our controller uses the four variables A, B, C and D, see figure 4.1. The most important variable is A, and it is also referred to as the Accumulator or Accu for short. A is involved in all of the arithmetic operations and receives as well the calculation result. In addition, A is used for data transport. B is mainly needed for arithmetic operations. C and D can be used for temporary storage and will later be used for counting loops.

There are also the two analog inputs (AD1 and AD2) and a PWM output. The processed data is limited to 4 bit and is only accessible via variable A (A <= AD1, PWM <= A). Variable A can also be loaded directly with a number from 0 to F via the 4n command. To load B, C or D, you must first load A, and then transfer the contents to the other registers via commands 51, 52, 53. Using A and B, some computations (commands 71 ...7A) can be performed.

Commands 40...4F load A with a new value, so 4n.

Instruction group 51...5A transfers the contents of A to a destination such as another variable or to the PWM output. In this group there are also commands to set a single bit of the output port, leaving the other 3 output bits unchanged.

Data transfers into A are done using 61 .. 6A, where source data is read into A. Instruction group 71...7A finally performs some arithmetic operations, and the result will always appear in variable A. The output port Dout includes the four outputs O1 to O4, which can be addressed together or as individual bits Dout.0 to Dout.3, so either as nibble or bitwise. The same applies to the inputs E1 to E4 that are used either as nibble or as four separate bits.

40...4F: Load A with a number from 0 to F

51...5F: Transfer the nibble in A to B, C, D, Dout, Dout.1, Dout.2, Dout.3, or PWM

51: B <= A

52: C <= A

53: D <= A

54: Dout <= A

55: Dout.0 <= A.0

56: Dout.1 <= A.0

57: Dout.2 <= A.0

58: Dout.3 <= A.0

59: PWM <= A

61...6A: the invers of 5, from B, C, D, Din, Din.0, Din.1, Din.2, Din.3, AD1, AD2 into A

61: A <= B

62: A <= C

63: A <= D

64: A <= Din

65: A <= Din.0

66: A <= Din.1

67: A <= Din.2

68: A <= Din.3

69: A <= AD1

6A: A <= AD2

71 ...7A: A <= instruction 7, with data 1...10, maths and logic

71: A <= A + 1

72: A <= A - 1

73: A <= A + B

74: A <= A - B

75: A <= A * B
76: A <= A / B
77: A <= A AND B
78: A <= A OR B
79: A <= A XOR B
7A: A <= NOT A

See listing 2.2, where you have used some of these instructions already. In listing 4.5 you can find the same program just starting from address 00 and a bit expanded. Start clean by setting the contents of A to 0; then increment A by one and send the contents of A to the LEDs, and as well to PWM output. You will get the increasing brightness on the PWM LED and as well an analog ramp signal at the D/A output if the RC network is still connected; it definitely is on my breadboard.

Then wait for 100ms and jump back to the beginning and increment, show on LEDs and PWM ...
Just by going through the comments, you can easily follow the program.

Address	Instruction	Data	Comment
00	4	0	A <= 0
01	7	1	A <= A + 1
02	5	4	Port <= A
03	5	9	PWM <= A
04	2	6	Wait for 100 ms
05	3	4	Jump to - 4

Program code: 40 71 54 59 26 34

Listing 4.5: Increment by one, show on LEDs and PWM

Listing 4.6 is another example, shown before in section 2.3, but now you will be able to understand it. Reading through the comments will give you already all of the explanations you need to see what happens. If you are not sure, look at figure 4.1b or 4.1c, fill in the data in each block and follow it one instruction after the other and see how the data is changed and transferred.

Address	Instruction	Data	Comment
00	6	9	A <= AD1
01	5	4	Port <= A
02	7	A	A <= Not A
03	5	9	PWM <= A
04	2	6	Wait 100 ms
05	3	5	Jump to - 5

Program code: 69 54 7A 59 26 35

Listing 4.6: Inverting the contents of A

As you can see there is an additional instruction at address 02, inverting the contents of A and see what the effect is.

4.3 - Jumps and Skips

Until now, the only way to change the sequential flow of the program was to jump back (THRow, so it must be instruction 3n). You could jump back by 0 (jump back to the same location you are now) to max 15 addresses back in your program. It would be nice to jump to any place in the 128 address space that we have available. But there are unfortunately only 4 bits available as our jump address, covering a range of max. 16 locations. The larger processors had a similar problem to extend the address range in the past, so a solution was found called paging.

It sounds difficult, but you actually use it every day: you call it the decimal system: we only have the numbers 0 to 9 available but want to define larger numbers. After 9 the next one is 10, but change it slightly and it becomes clearer: 09 then 10, so page 0 for 00-09, page 1 10-19 and so on, until you reach 99, the end of page 9. Using this system, we can define 100 locations in decimal by just using number 0 to 9.

Transfer the same principle to hexadecimal and we solved our problem: we start with the high nibble at 0 and can cover the 16 locations from 00 to 0F, then continue with 10 to 1F, 20 to 2F and so on, max up to FF. As we only have 128 addresses to cover in our EEPROM, our max is 7F, so pages 0 to 7 are enough.
We introduce a paging register. Whenever we want to be free where to jump, we use two instructions: 8n (n=0-7) to preset a page to jump to and then the actual Jump instruction 9n. As shown in figure 4.1a, the page and the jump address are combined to form the full 3bit + 4bit jump address. Make sure this page is preset correctly, before the Jump instruction 9 is executed. So you set the page you want to jump to first, then later you do your Jump and the bits are automatically combined. After a Reset the page number is automatically set to page 0. And without setting the page first to another number, the Jump instruction executes on page 0, so jump area 00 to 0F.

The other way of influencing the program flow is by using the Skip instructions Cn. If the condition specified in the instruction is met, the next instruction is skipped over, if not met the next instruction is executed. Let's look at what happens using listing 2.4, I copied it further down so you do not have to search.
You can describe your program flow using such a flow chart and you can see, if condition is met (Y), you jump over the next location, if not met, you execute it.

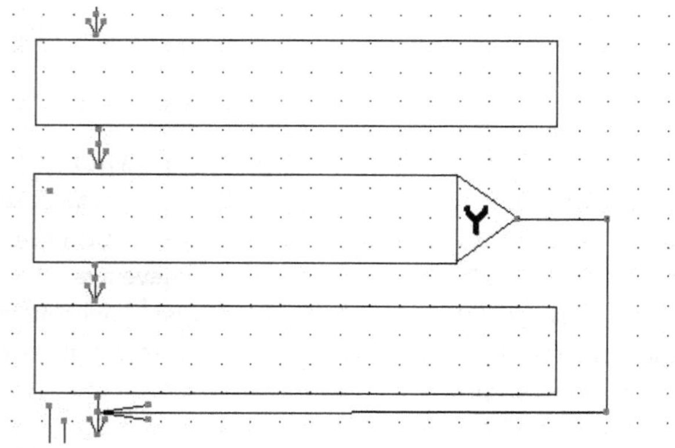

Flowchart 1: Do a test, **SKIP over if Yes**, else next instruction

If the condition in the instruction is not met, continue and execute as normal
If condition is met though, then exit at Y, and skip over next instruction.

There are not many parts you need with this processor to do a flow chart:
The block, the skip unit, and back to the jump location for now.

A quick walk through the program: Display the contents of A on the LEDs, then check if S1 is 1 (open), so if S1 not pushed, the program skips over the increment A and nothing changes as the contents of A stays the same. As soon as S1 is 0, the Skip is not executed but A is incremented, a jump back and the display is updated until S1 is open again, and the random number does not change anymore.

Altogether there are 15 possible Skip Instructions with different conditions for register A/B comparisons, input bits, S1 and S2.

Address	Instruction	Data	Comment
30	5	4	Port <= A
31	C	E	S1 = 1?
32	7	1	A<= A + 1
33	3	3	Jump to - 3

Listing 2.4: Random Number Generator

Another way to change the sequential flow of a program is to call subroutines. Let's assume you have a function like: get data from the input - multiply by 2 - output to LEDs, 10 times in your program. You can shorten your program by defining 64, 75 (with 2 in B), 54 as subroutine. This block has 3 bytes, x10 executed = 30 bytes of code in your program. 10 subroutine calls cost 10 Call instructions, you need to add a Return instruction at the end of the subroutine block to come back, so from the 3 to a 4 instruction block 64 75 54 E0, together 10+4=14 bytes and you save 30 – 14=16 bytes in your program.

Calling a subroutine is defined as nesting. Theoretically you could have this subroutine call another subroutine, and so you would have many levels of nesting. But each time you have to memorize somewhere, which address to jump back to after your subroutine has finished. As our little MyCo has limited resources, only one level of nesting is allowed, so our main program can only call one subroutine at the time, but you can have many different subroutine calls as you like, but have to return before you call the next one. Or said differently: you can memorize one return address.

But how does this subroutine mechanism work?
Think of flight of stairs and a stack of plates next to it, and one additional plate that is easy to access. After 6 steps you decide to go into the room on the right, but you want to be sure you can continue where the next step would have been, which is 7, so you write 7 on the empty plate and put it onto the stack. Our Interpreter does the

same, saving this address 7 in RAM. If you were to find another distraction in this room (go to another subroutine), you would overwrite the 7 you had memorized, and as there is only one storage location, you could never come back to 7.

To overcome such a problem, bigger processors use a so called stack, a block of memory locations. Just imagine this pile of plates which is your working area and another few plates not on the pile. Let's go back to our flight of stairs. You are on step number 6 and want to go in another direction. The next one you want to use is 7, so you write 7 on an unused plate and put it on top of the stack you have.

Next time at a detour you write the next return address onto a plate, add it to the pile before executing the subroutine. As long as you have enough unused plates you can add to the pile, it can grow. On the way back you always look at the top plate, take it off the stack, showing the next return location. Having come back via all of the return addresses, you end up with a plate and number 7 on it, and this is where you want to continue your main program.

The Instructions used in this context are a subroutine call (Call) and the associated return instruction (Return). But remember, this Interpreter can memorize only one return address.

Now more Instructions explained:

80 ... 8F: Program the paging register, the high nibble of our Jump address, Addr high = 0...7

90 ... 9F: Direct Jump to 128 bytes, High nibble page addr and Low nibble in Jump Instruction

A0 ... AF: Counting loop C times Addr high, Addr low (0...15)

B0 ... BF: Counting loop D times Addr high, Addr low (0...15)

C1 ... CF: Conditional Jumps: If (condition 1...15) is met, then skip the next instruction

C1: if A> B then Addr = Addr + 1

C2: if A <B then Addr = Addr + 1

C3: if A = B then Addr = Addr + 1

C4: if Din.0 = 1 then Addr = Addr + 1

C5: if Din.1 = 1 then Addr = Addr + 1

C6: if Din.2 = 1 then Addr = Addr + 1

C7: if Din.3 = 1 then Addr = Addr + 1

C8: if Din.0 = 0 then Addr = Addr + 1
C9: if Din.1 = 0 then Addr = Addr + 1
CA: if Din.2 = 0 then Addr = Addr + 1
CB: if Din.3 = 0 then Addr = Addr + 1

CC: if S1 = 0 then Addr = Addr + 1
CD: if S2 = 0 then Addr = Addr + 1

CE: if S1 = 1 then Addr = Addr + 1
CF: if S2 = 1 then Addr = Addr + 1

D0 ... DF: Subroutine call Addr high, Addr low (0...15), (Call)
E0 ... EF: Return from subroutine, (Return)

An example of the use of such a conditional Jump instruction can be found in our example program in chapter 2.6. It has been slightly modified here to start at address 00. As the upper part of the address (Addr high) in the paging register is 0 after Reset, instruction 80 is not needed here. As before, the length of the key down is measured and displayed. In this example here, all wait commands have been removed from the program, and it now operates at a higher resolution.

Address	Instruction	Data	Comment
00	C	C	S1 = 0?
01	3	1	Jump to - 1
02	4	0	A <= 0
03	7	1	A <= A + 1
04	5	4	Port <= A
05	C	E	S1 = 1?
06	3	3	Jump to - 3
07	3	7	Jump to - 7

CC 31 40 71 54 CE 33 37

Listing 4.7: S1 button response with higher resolution

The Jump instruction CC at address 00 evaluates the status of switch S1. In the resting state, S1 = 1, then the condition is not true and the instruction at address 01 is not skipped, the relative jump instruction to -1 is executed. The program repeats this command sequence in address 00 and 01, until the button is pressed. Then, the condition becomes true and the address 01 is skipped over and instruction 40 at address 02 is executed. Thus, the actual measuring process begins.

The Accu is set to 00, then incremented by 1, the result output to the LEDs. At the address 05 you find another conditional Jump command, CE. Here the Skip condition is for S1 = 1, check if S1 released. As the button was initially pressed, the condition is not true in the beginning. The command in 06 is therefore executed and leads to a return to -3, going through another increment loop starting at address 03. Only when the button is released, the program proceeds to address 07 and thus a return to the beginning and the LED display stays stable.

Enter the program and test it. The reaction time is measured with higher resolution now compared to the older program. The resolution time is now about 5ms.
And do not forget, the original example program is still in memory starting at address 34h, only the lower bytes at addresses 00 to 07 have been overwritten. Write a small program that contains only a jump to this start address 34.

As the start address is not on page 0 but on page 3, we must first set the paging register to 3. The subsequent absolute jump to the specified address 4 then takes us actually to 34, not to 04. A bit confusing sometimes, and this is where the programming pages help, as you can see which value is stored where.

Address	Instruction	Data	Comment
00	8	3	Set to page 3
01	9	4	Jump to Address = x4

83 94

Listing 4.8: Absolute Jump to pre-programmed timer program

After Reset the original example program at address 34 is called. You can test the same behaviour for other examples. The complete listing of all available programs and subroutines you can find in the Appendix.

4.4 - The Instruction Table

As we have seen all of the instructions now, here the overview in the form of an Instruction Table. The top row shows the instruction number 1 to E, and underneath all of the up to 16 variants. A copy of this table you can find as well in the Appendix.

	1	2	3	4	5	6	7	8	9	A	B	C	D	E
	to Port	Wait	Jump back	A<= ...	... <=A	A<= ...	A<= ...	Set Page	Jump (Page)	C*	D*	Skip if ...	Call	Ret
0	0	1 ms	0	0				0	0	0	0		0	
1	1	2 ms	1	1	B<=A	A<= B	A<=A+1	1	1	1	1	A>B	1	
2	2	5 ms	2	2	C<=A	A<=C	A<=A-1	2	2	2	2	A<B	2	
3	3	10	3	3	D<=A	A<=D	A<=A+B	3	3	3	3	A=B	3	
4	4	20	4	4	Dout<=A	A<=Din	A<=A-B	4	4	4	4	Din.0=1	4	
5	5	50	5	5	A.0	A<=Din.0	A<= A*B	5	5	5	5	Din.1=1	5	
6	6	100	6	6	A.0	A<=Din.1	A<=A/B	6	6	6	6	Din.2=1	6	
7	7	200	7	7	A.0	A<=Din.2	B	7	7	7	7	Din.3=1	7	
8	8	500	8	8	A.0	A<=Din.3	A<=A Or B		8	8	8	Din.0=0	8	
9	9	1 s	9	9	PWM<=A	A<=AD1	A<= A Xor		9	9	9	Din.1=0	9	
A	10	2 s	10	10		A<=AD2	A<=Not A		A	A	A	Din.2=0	A	
B	11	5 s	11	11					B	B	B	Din.3=0	B	
C	12	10 s	12	12					C	C	C	S1=0	C	
D	13	20 s	13	13					D	D	D	S2=0	D	
E	14	30 s	14	14					E	E	E	S1=1	E	
F	15	60 s	15	15					F	F	F	S2=1	F	

5 – Program Structures and Sample Programs

Many easy to understand examples have been presented in the first chapters. As you have seen the complete Instruction Table now, you can probably understand better what is going on in these programs. Just go back and follow the program flow, checking with the Instruction Table.

Now we will show more possibilities and as well more complex program structures. They are not only used here with MyCo, but are used in any programming language, so they could be implemented in a similar way in Assembler, Basic, C or Forth. Thus, the methods shown here go beyond the application of MyCo and are basic structures applicable to other systems.

Programming exercises with MyCo will therefore help you to start with the basics, before you get into complex processors and programming, especially to mention Arduino and Raspberry Pi, where so many boards are available at low cost. One of the most important issues is the availability of low cost hardware nowadays. MyCo is a starting point for PC independent programming, but there are possibilities as well to connect MyCo to a PC, but more about this later.

5.1 - Counting Loops

Delay loops are needed very often, as you have seen in the previous examples. Rather than programming this each time we want to have a block ready that we can just use, like a subroutine. We use register C as a loop counter.
Get 5 into A, transfer to C. Then the main program to set port to 0101, delay for 500ms, send 1010 to the LEDs, delay another 500ms, set page to 0.

The A2 command performs an absolute jump to address 02 and reduces at the same time the contents of variable C by one. If the contents of register C has reached zero, the jump is not performed and the program continues to address 08 and stops by jumping to the same address. Reset, to start all over. The absolute jump address always refers to the specified page. With this program here on page 0, the command 80 could be omitted. But if the jump is to another page, the page register has to be set before. Go back to figure 4.1, there you see all of the internals in one row. Copy it onto a page of paper, write the instructions in there and see how the internals react – a small debugger. Like in the appendix, 16 times the same line. This will make it a lot clearer for you. And you can basically run MyCo without having one, Instruction Table and Programming page should be sufficient.

Address	Instruction	Data	Comment
00	4	5	A <= 5
01	5	2	C <= A
02	1	5	Port <= 0101
03	2	8	Wait 500 ms
04	1	A	Port <= 1010
05	2	8	Wait 500 ms
06	8	0	Set to Page 0
07	A	2	C times 02
08	3	0	End

45 52 15 28 1A 28 80 A2 30

Listing 5.1: A timing loop

Test this program. The LEDs in each pass will show the pattern 0101 and 1010. However it will take 6 runs and not 5 as we wanted, as we set the counter to 05, then do the first pattern, before the counting down starts, so 1+5. So change the counting variable at address 01 to 4 and test again. Now the LEDs will just blink five times.

In the next example 5.2, we will not jump back as in listing 5.1, but jump forward. This time the blinking is actually carried out five times, as we do this within the loop. Instruction A5 skips over the end instruction 30 if not 0, if 0 just continues to address 04 with 30, a jump 0 addresses away, so the same address and stops in this infinite loop. This time the end of the program is actually not at the end.

Address	Instruction	Data	Comment
00	4	5	A <= 5
01	5	2	C <= A
02	8	0	AddrHi <=0
03	A	5	C-times 05, skip if not 0
04	3	0	End

05	1	5	Port <= 0101
06	2	8	Wait for 500 ms
07	1	A	Port <= 1010
08	2	8	Wait for 500 ms
09	3	6	Jump to - 6

45 52 80 A5 30 15 28 1A 28 36

Listing 5.2: Five times flashing

5.2 - Compare Instructions

Compare instructions can only be done with A and B involved, as A>B, A<B and A=B. As before, the next instruction is skipped if Yes, otherwise just proceeds to the next instruction. Depending on the result of the comparison, a skip is executed. In the following example register B is preloaded with the number 5. Register A gets the result from the analog input AD1. Here it could be connected to a light sensor as described in chapter 2.4. This program will now continuously perform the following action:

First get the number 5 into A,
then transfer it to B.
Set page register to 0
and start the loop:

If AD1 > 5

Then: switch all LEDs on
Otherwise: all LEDs off

The end result of this program is basically a light level switched LED. As the LDR is connected to GND, more brightness leads to a smaller voltage at the input of AD1. The LEDs are switched off as soon as a certain brightness is exceeded, and thus a certain voltage is reached. The switching limit is the value 6, because the measurement result must be greater than 5.

Address	Instruction	Data	Comment
00	4	5	A <= 5
01	5	1	B <= A
02	8	0	AddrHi = 0
03	6	9	A <= AD1
04	C	1	Skip if A>B
05	9	8	Page Addr 08
06	1	F	LEDs 1111
07	3	4	Jump to Addr 03
08	1	0	Set LEDs to 0000
09	3	6	Addr 03, 6 back

45 51 80 69 C1 98 1F 34 10 36

Listing 5.3: Simple twilight switch

Test the program and play with your lighting conditions and with the setting of B to other values than 5, for example shade the light sensor with your hand slowly to see what happens. You will see that the basic function of a twilight switch is executed. However, there will be a difficult area when the system is at the switching point between on and off, and the LEDs might flicker. This can happen especially with fluorescent lighting where the light level switches rapidly - too fast for your eyes but not for this controller - the system measures the light level of the LDR. This wavering is then actually correctly evaluated by the program, but the result is not as you would expect from a dimmer switch. An improved twilight switch taking care of this is shown in chapter 6.1, and will be explained in detail there.

5.3 - Single Bit Processing

Until now we have used the numbers 0 to F to describe inputs and outputs, and as well the PWM output shows 16 levels, all data worked on in nibbles. But if a system uses switches as inputs, lamps and relays for outputs for example, a logic functionality has to be processed. Then you have to change to processing individual bits, like in a PLC - Programmable Logic Controller.

The basic logic functions are:

INVERT where A = NOT B. You would use this to change the polarity of a signal, e.g. what is happening at an Input switch in the example 5.1. You might want to change polarity. For now the not active switch signal is one, as the internal resistor pulls it High. You might want to define that switch on (0) is active, High, the INVERT would take the low signal and invert it to High for further processing.

AND - both inputs have to be High to set the output to 1. Example: Kids Fran AND John have to sit in the car to take them both to school, if only one is there, you have to wait with status 0.

OR - either of the two inputs is sufficient at 1 to change the output to 1. Example: either of the parents can drive them to school.

EXOR - means Exclusive OR, and excludes the both from the OR above, basically meaning either mom or dad can drive the car, but not both at the same time.

The following program reads in the state of the line Din.2 so input In3, which can be High or Low. The read command 67 in line 00 returns either the value 0 or 1 into Accumulator A, depending on the switch status. As you know already, the inputs are all pulled to High via an internal resistor in the IC, so an open input is read as High. Closing the switch, leads to a Low at the Input. Thus, the LED is turned off or on at output A3 accordingly. All other LEDs remain switched off.

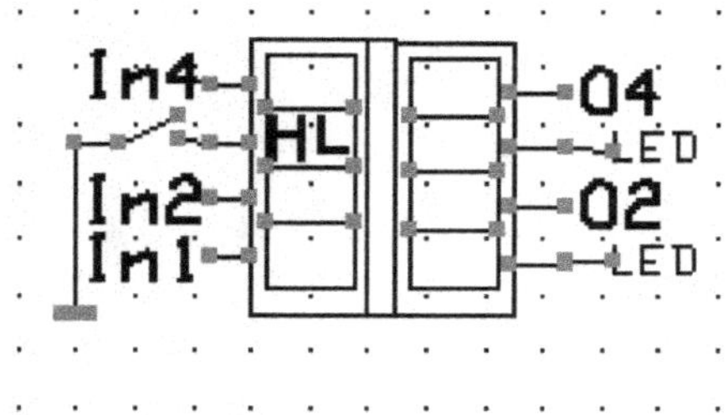

Figure 5.1: Testing of E3/In3/Din.2

Just a quick explanation regarding names/numbers on inputs and outputs. I want to keep my definitions as close to what is printed onto the PCB, and in the Instruction Table, and in the original German booklet; so you get E1, E2, E3 and E4 as there are 4 Inputs as printed on the PCB. In computing, the numbers run from 0 to x, so here from 0, to 1, 2 and 3 as in the Instruction Table. If you look at the Instruction Table, it is used in exactly this way, 65 to 68 related to Din.0, Din.1, Din.2 and Din.3, identical to E1, E2, E3 and E4.

The same inconsistency actually appears on the outputs, and for easy reading a third numbering is added; so on the PCB you find outputs A1, A2, A3 and A4; look at instructions 55 to 58, there it is Dout.0, Dout.1, Dout.2 and Dout.3. And to help you to read a hexadecimal number at the output using 4 LEDs, the LEDs connected to these 4 outputs are numbered 8, 4, 2, 1, just add up the numbers on the LEDs switched on, for example 4 on, 2 on and 1 on adds up to 7 in hexadecimal; 8 on, 2 on means A, see as well the conversion table in the Appendix. I had to decide where to use the original and where other notations. I tried to make it the easiest for understanding. Now back to bits.

Input 3 = Din.2 is High when the switch open, Low when switch closed. My setup on the prototype board and the DIL switch makes it easy to test for me, all inputs are immediately available to modify the input level. If the DIL switch is in the off position, another external signal could actually be connected without removing the DIL switch, in technical terms you would call such a connectivity a wired OR, as either the DIL switch or the additional input can be used to bring the signal to Low.

Be careful though, as the forgotten DIL at Low, switched to ground could cause a problem: always have a resistor in series with the external input to avoid issues, because your DIL switch could short circuit your external input – the resistor will avoid causing trouble to the external signal, but the DIL might still shorten the signal and give a wrong reading of the actual input signal.

Address	**Instruction**	**Data**	**Comment**
00	6	7	A <= Din.2 (E3)
01	5	4	Port <= A
02	2	1	Wait 2 ms
03	3	3	Jump to - 3

67 54 21 33

Listing 5.4: Single bit testing and display

Program in this code and run it; looking at the comments you will easily understand what is happening:

After reset, the input is open, so input High, the processor looks at E3, and a value is transferred into A with A=1 if open and A=0 with switch closed - LED O1 will react accordingly. Then there is a short delay loop of 2ms and a jump back to the beginning of the program. The other 3 programs to read inputs are 65 54 21 33 for In1, 66 54 21 33 for In2, and 68 54 21 33 for In4. Test the other inputs as well by moving your connection to ground or just close another one of the DIL switches.

In the same way as we have now looked at the status of the 4 inputs, you can as well route the result of the bit value to any of the 4 LEDs. See listing 5.5. It controls the output Port.2 = A3. There are 5 instructions to do output: 54 sends the 4 bit contents of A - all 4 bits to all 4 LEDs, so the full nibble; 55 routes the status of A.0 to LED 0, 56 to LED 1, 57 to LED 4 and 58 to LED 8. The LED on output A3 looks at bit 0 in A flashes at a frequency of about 1Hz when the lowest bit is 1, so all odd input numbers 1, 3 , ...
500ms LED on and 500ms LED off.

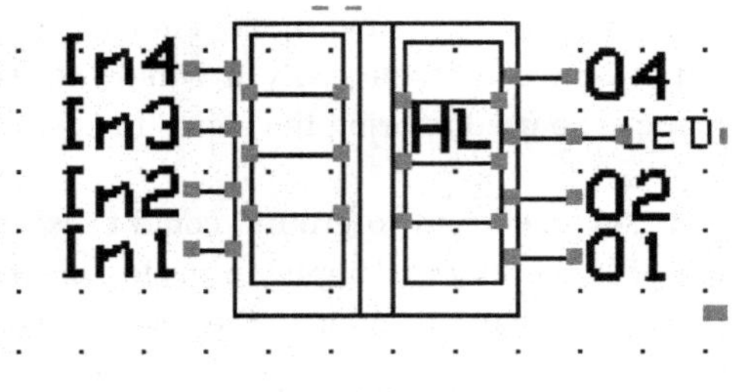

Figure 5.2: Controlling output A3/O3

Address	Instruction	Data	Comment
00	7	1	A <= A + 1
01	5	7	Port.2 <= A.0
02	2	8	Wait for 500 ms
03	3	3	Jump to - 3

71 57 28 33

Listing 5.5: A blinking LED on A3/O3/4

An input bit can be copied and inverted, then sent to any output via the A register. It would then inverted indicate 1 as switch is closed, and 0 as switch not activated. The following program takes the input bit, inverts the bit state in the Accumulator and sends the result to A4. If the input is High, the LED is off; and the output A4 changes to High, when the 0 is applied to input E3, for example meaning the DIL switch changes the input to Low.

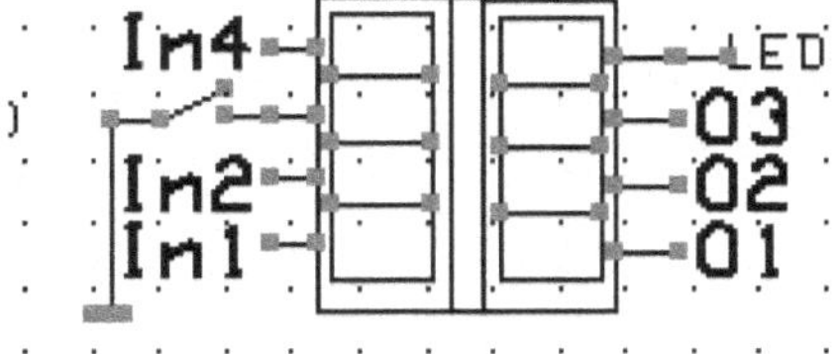

Figure 5.3: Inverted output

Address	Instruction	Data	Comment
00	6	7	A <= Din.2
01	7	A	A = NOT A
02	5	8	Port.3 <= A.0
03	3	3	Jump to - 3

67 7A 58 33

Listing 5.6: Invert a single bit and copy to O4/Port.3

Another type of single bit processing uses the SKIP instructions to test various conditions, see C4 to CF. Depending on the state of a single bit tested Yes, the next instruction is skipped. Similar commands have been used already for S1/S2 status testing.

In this example we use E3 and E4. If E3 is High, the next instruction is skipped over and there is no output, the status of the output register stays unchanged. The same, if E4 stays High when tested.

However, if one of the 2 inputs is switched to GND, the relevant nibble is sent to the output register of the LEDs. For output A1 for example this means that E4 is a reset (Reset, R) and for E3 Low (Set, S). Hence the function of an RS flip-flop is simulated, one output is 0 and the other one is 1.

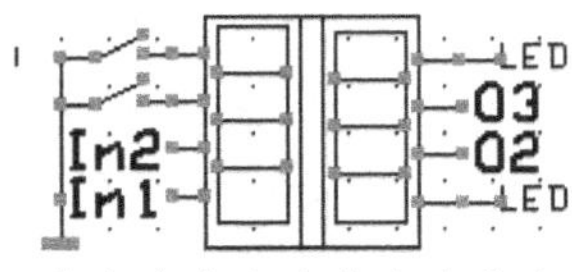

Figure 5.4: Change over switch with two outputs

Address	Instruction	Data	Comment
00	C	6	Skip if Din.2=1
01	1	1	Port <= 1 (0001)
02	C	7	Skip if Din.3=1
03	1	8	Port <= 8 (1000)
04	3	4	Go to Addr = 0

C6 11 C7 18 34

Listing 5.7: An RS flip-flop (Reset and Set)

5.4 - Basic Logic Functions

Here the implemented logic functions in more detail. We only look at the 2 input versions. (The same rules apply if more inputs are used, 3 to n inputs). For AND all inputs have to be High, for OR one of the n inputs has to be High, to set the output to High. In other words, two binary inputs can be linked to a new output state.

As first example the AND function: When bit x has the state 1 AND bit y has the 1 state, the output state is also 1.

AND	X	Y	Result
	0	0	0
	0	1	0
	1	0	0
	1	1	1

The following program combines the input states with the number 3 (0011). The AND function means in this case, that only the lower 2 bits are looked at, basically the two lower bits masked in, the higher 2 bits are filtered out. With all inputs open, the inputs are pulled to High by internal resistors, so the input state is 1111. The AND operation with 0011 then provides results of the 2 lower inputs to the LEDs.

As said, the lower 2 bits are masked in, and if these 2 inputs change to 0, the outputs on O1 and O2 follow. Outputs O3 and O4 stay Low as masked out, independent of the relevant input status. So AND is here used for masking, and not to execute a logic function on a bit, as before.

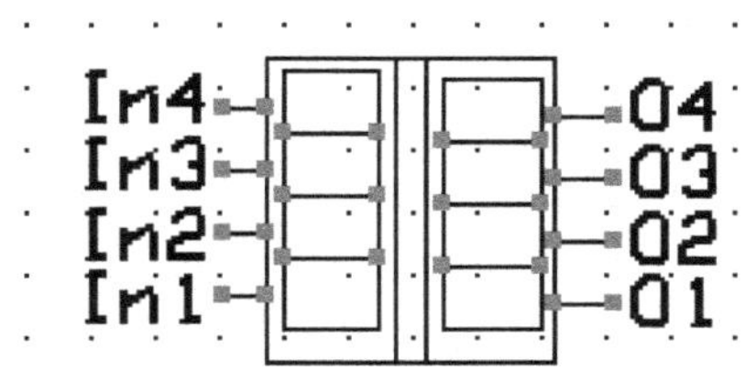

Figure 5.6: The four inputs E1...E4 (In1...In4) and 4 outputs A1...A4 (O1...O4), ANDing with 0011 Masking bit 0 and 1 in, masking bit 2 and 3 out

Address	Instruction	Data	Comment
00	6	4	A <= Din
01	5	1	B <= A
02	4	3	A <= 3 (0011)
03	7	7	A<= A AND B
04	5	4	Port <= A
05	3	5	Jump to - 5

64 51 43 77 54 35

Listing 5.8: Implementation of the AND function to mask bits

Now the OR function: as you can see, any input or both set to 1 sets the output to 1, independent of the other input. This can be used to set any output in our nibble to 1, independent of the input value of the others.

OR	X	Y	Result
	0	0	0
	0	1	1
	1	0	1
	1	1	1

Using the XOR function (A=A XOR B, 79), you can invert any individual bits in our nibble.
1111 XOR 0010 would give 1101, just changing the value of this one bit.

XOR	X	Y	Result
	0	0	0
	0	1	1
	1	0	1
	1	1	0

And just for completeness the logic of inverting a signal.

INVERT		Y	Result
		0	1
		1	0

For example, to be used to change the open input signal High to not active Low for further processing, and in the same way the Low input of a button to be switched to a High output signal.

5.5 - Subroutines

Until now we had our programs mainly go through the instructions one by one until the end and then start executing from the beginning again. Now to the use of subroutines in more detail. We explained it a bit before, but now we will show how it works including example programs.

Certain instruction blocks of a program are the same and will be used many times, so you have two options: either you will keep it as is and it will run faster or you decide to introduce the use of subroutines; slightly slower, but saving code space. And as we only have 128 bytes this looks like a good idea.
Basically, if you are the main program, you hire somebody new and give them this piece of work that has to be repeated many times. This special piece of code will stay elsewhere as one piece and will be called when needed. You run the main code up to this point, say CALL SUBx and your new colleague does his/her bit. This could be many different activities, but as explained before, only one at the time.

At the end the relevant subroutine will be a DONE / RET and you continue with your main work. The 2 Instructions D (Call) and E (Return) are introduced here again in more detail.

The designed inline code without subroutines will for example contain this piece of code 10 times. Let's assume it consists of 5 bytes, so 10x5 = 50 byte of inline code; more than one third of the code space we have. To use subroutines you have to add a CALL instruction in the main program each time = 10 bytes, and as well the subroutine block has to come back to the main program via a Return instruction at the end of this block of code, so now 5+1=6 byte; 10 bytes CALL plus 1 byte return in the subroutine, extending the subroutine to 6 bytes 10 + 6 = 16 bytes, saving 34 bytes, or counted differently, about two thirds of this part of the code.

It does not seem much, but if you run out of code space left in your EEPROM - life saving. The following example demonstrates the use of a subroutine that is invoked in two places by the main program. The subroutine in this case contains only one statement (A = A - 1) and the return instruction. Therefore, it does not save much memory space here, but the example is only used to demonstrate the CALL instruction and the RET instruction.

Look as well at instruction 80 at address 00, which ensures that the page is set to 0.

Main program:

Address	**Instruction**	**Data**	**Comment**
00	8	0	AddrHi <=0
01	D	8	Call 08
02	5	4	Dout <= A
03	2	9	Wait for 1 s
04	D	8	Call 08
05	5	4	Dout <= A
06	2	8	Wait for 0,5 s
07	3	7	Jump to - 7

Subroutine:

Address	Instruction	Data	Comment
08	7	2	A <= A - 1
09	E	0	Return

80 D8 54 29 D8 54 28 37 72 E0 as main and sub follow each other in code space

Listing 5.9: Main program and subroutine calls

The result of this program is a descending binary counter with different time delays. Also try other instructions in this subroutine or extend it.

The Holtek chip comes pre-loaded with sample programs as well as with several useful subroutines, that can be called by your own programs. The complete code is fully documented in the Appendix.

For your own use you must only know the entry address of the relevant functionality:

Subroutine at address:
50: this produces a long sound
52: this delivers a short sound
53: generates a variable length sound, length in A
60: wait for key press of S1
68: wait for key press of S2
70: input a number using S1 and S2
The subroutine at address 60 will now be used to build a counter that is controlled by the S1 button.

The count begins with zero. The main program is relatively short because the complex task of switch query is executed by the subroutine, so invisible, except for the call at address 04.

Address	Instruction	Data	Comment
00	4	0	A <= 0
01	5	4	Dout <= A
02	7	1	A <= A + 1
03	8	6	Set to Page 6
04	D	0	Call 60 to read S1
05	3	4	Jump to - 4

40 54 71 86 D0 34

Listing 5.10: Counter, controlled via S1

Test the program. If you press S1 ten times, the result should be 1010. The counter value is displayed via the LEDs as well.

Now modify this program to use the subroutine at address 68. Well, now the counter responds to S2.

6 - Advanced Applications

Many of the previous program examples could be already used in applications. In this chapter we will extend this - mostly more complex and building on what we know already about this MyCo controller. They can easily be adapted, changed and extended to suit your own specific control tasks and requirements.

6.1 - Twilight Switch

A twilight switch using our LDR light sensor had been shown already in listing 2.3. It is designed to switch on the lights when the ambient light falls below a certain threshold level; if it gets lighter, to turn the external light off again. The problem we had found was the transition point, the switching point.

It should be ensured, that the light does not flicker on the border between light and dark. This is achieved now using a so called hysteresis between on and off, i.e. a certain difference of the switching levels when it comes on or when it goes off. The program presented here will work according to the following rules:

> If the voltage at AD1 is not less than level 9, the LED is turned on. (Dark)
> If the voltage at AD1 is not greater than level 5, the LED is turned off. (Light)

As such this controller has a middle region, where no change of the output state will happen. This area prevents the flickering of the LEDs that we had experienced before.

0 1 2 3 4 5	LEDs off
6 7 8:	LEDs unchanged and this applies to getting lighter and as well getting darker
9 A B C D E F	LEDs on

Address	Instruction	Data	Comment
00	1	0	Set LEDs to 0000
01	4	5	A <= 5
02	5	1	B <= A
03	6	9	A <= AD1
04	C	1	Skip if A>B
05	1	0	Set LEDs to 0000
06	4	9	A <= 9
07	5	1	B <= A
08	6	9	A <= AD1
09	C	2	Skip if A<B
0A	1	F	Set LEDs to 1111
0B	3	A	Jump to -10 =01

10 45 51 69 C1 10 49 51 69 C2 1F 3A

Listing 6.1: Twilight switch with hysteresis

Type it in, test it and change the hysteresis points, to adapt the behaviour to your local light conditions.

6.2 - Two Point Controller

A simple thermostat, for example, as in an iron, works as a two level controller. There are two predefined temperatures at which the heating element is either switched on or switched off to keep a constant temperature. Between these two points there is a hysteresis as well. It provides, for example, a temperature of 80 degrees and achieves an actual temperature profile, which varies between 78° C and 82° C.

Such a two-position controller can be reproduced here as a model. Instead of a temperature, this is simulated by a voltage across a capacitor in our example. The voltage level required (temperature defined) is set via AD1, for example via the 10k resistor and the LDR we have, or via an additional potentiometer simulating the temperature setting (not part of thit kit). AD2 measures the actual voltage at the capacitor, simulating the actual temperature.

When switched on, the capacitor is empty, so it will be charged until the voltage is higher than AD1. Then the output for charging will be changed from 1 (on) to 0 (off) and the capacitor is slowly discharged. The capacitor is always either charged or discharged a little via a resistor attached to A4 to keep a constant voltage. If you have access to a scope, you can see the ramping up, and from then on the triangular change around the set voltage (temperature) as average. Dependent on the result of the comparison, you can see as well on the LED if the capacitor is charged (1000) or discharged (0000) via the 10k resistor.

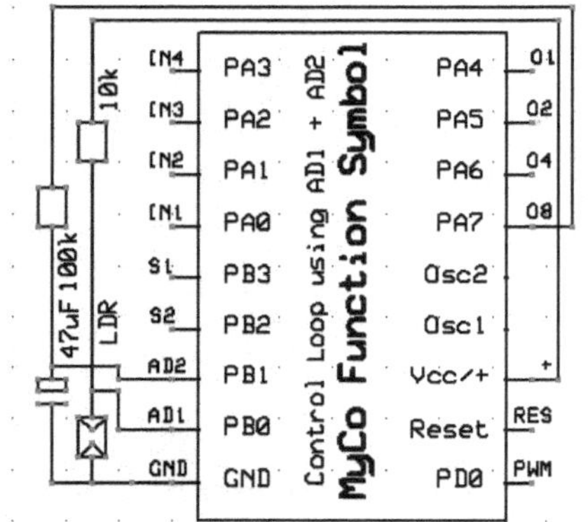

Figure 6.1: Control loop using AD2

Figure 6.2: Voltage control via AD2

This control process requires the smallest hysteresis possible to be as accurate as possible. Without special measures, a hysteresis result of one step of the AD converter can be achieved, so you can see the hysteresis of about 0.3V at 4.5V supply voltage. In operation, you can see a rapid flickering of the LED on A4 until stable.

If any change in the lighting conditions happens, this is like changing the requested temperature. The nominal voltage at the LDR changes at the input of AD1, and the control loop will follow with a certain delay, until the actual voltage across the electrolytic capacitor is about the same as AD1 input.

Address	Instruction	Data	Comment
00	6	9	A <= AD1
01	5	1	B <= A
02	8	0	AddrHi <= 0
03	6	A	A<=AD2
04	C	1	Skip if A>B
05	9	8	Addr 08
06	1	0	Output 0000
07	3	7	Jump to - 7
08	1	8	Output 1000
09	3	9	Jump to - 9

69 51 80 6A C1 98 10 37 18 39

Listing 6.2: The voltage follow loop

6.3 - LED Dimmer

This example program of an LED dimmer uses S1 and S2 to increase and reduce the brightness on the PWM output. The LED on the PWM output represents the brightness level. For setting the desired level you can use two ways: a short push of the button increases or decreases the level by one, or you leave the finger on, and the brightness level changes continuously until the finger is removed or you have reached the upper or lower limit.

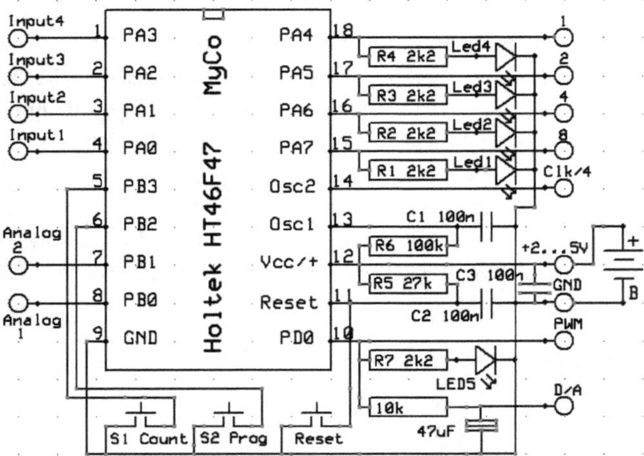

The 4 skip instructions need quite a bit of code space compared to the other examples we had before. Two of them are needed for checking if a switch is pressed, either S1 or S2. If Yes, then the brightness level is either increased or decreased. But as we keep increasing, after 15 steps the next level would be 0, so some check is required for max and min; or down to 0, the next one would be 15 - the value would wrap around as higher bits do not exist (overflow or underflow).

So, tests are required if Max (15) or Min (0) have been reached. As all of the skip testing and comparisons have to take place in register A, it has to be kept free and many of our instructions are just needed to save the contents of A into other registers. For this purpose, Variable C is used here.

Address	Instruction	Data	Comment
00	8	0	AddrHi <= 0
01	5	9	PWM <= A
02	2	7	Wait for 200 ms
03	5	2	C <= A
04	4	F	A <= 15
05	5	1	B <= A
06	6	2	A <= C
07	C	2	Skip if A<B
08	9	B	Jump to 0B
09	C	F	Skip if S2=1
0A	7	1	A <= A + 1
0B	5	2	C <= A

0C	4	0	A <= 0
0D	5	1	B <= A
0E	6	2	A <= C
0F	C	1	Skip if A>B
10	9	0	Jump to 00
11	C	E	Skip if S1 = 1
12	7	2	A <= A - 1
15	9	0	Jump to 00

80 59 27 52 4F 51 62 C2 9B CF 71 52 40 51 62 C1 90 CE 72 90

Listing 6.3: Brightness control

And we have exactly achieved what we wanted: increase and decrease brightness via S1 and S2, but additionally ensure that the minimum limit is 0 and the maximum limit is 15.

6.4 – Morse Code Program

To generate Morse code as sound, five parts of program are needed: a program to generate a sound, a timing loop to generate a short sound, a long sound, the pause between short and long, and the longer pause between Morse code letters/numbers. Our first guess would be to use the PWM output for sound, but unfortunately the PWM frequency is too high for this, so we have to find another solution.
Fortunately, there is a subroutine provided at address 50 already in our example programs that can be adapted.

The tone duration is determined by the D counting loop on a Call from address 53 with a maximum value of 15. An entry at address 52 would result in a short tone.
The following program largely corresponds to the subroutine starting at address 50. There is a difference though: at the end there is no return, but the usual 30 instructions, jumping back to the same location, so our endless loop, to get out of only with a Reset.

After a Reset, a single tone with a maximum length is generated. Try different settings of the waiting loop commands. The program is a compromise between long sustain and good audibility via the piezo transducer. The audio signal appears at the output A4. Connect the sounder between A4 and GND and listen.

Address	Instruction	Data	Comment
00	8	0	Set to page 0 >long
01	4	F	A <= 15
02	9	4	Jump to Addr 04
03	4	5	A <= 5 >short
04	5	3	D <= A >variable
05	1	8	Dout 8
06	1	0	Dout 0
07	2	1	Wait for 2 ms
08	1	8	Dout 8
09	1	0	Dout 0
0A	2	1	Wait for 2 ms
0B	1	8	Dout 8
0C	1	0	Dout 0
0D	2	0	Wait for 1 ms
0E	B	5	D * 5
0F	3	0	End here, stop

80 4F 94 45 53 18 10 21 18 10 21 18 10 20 B5 30

Listing 6.4: Test the sound output

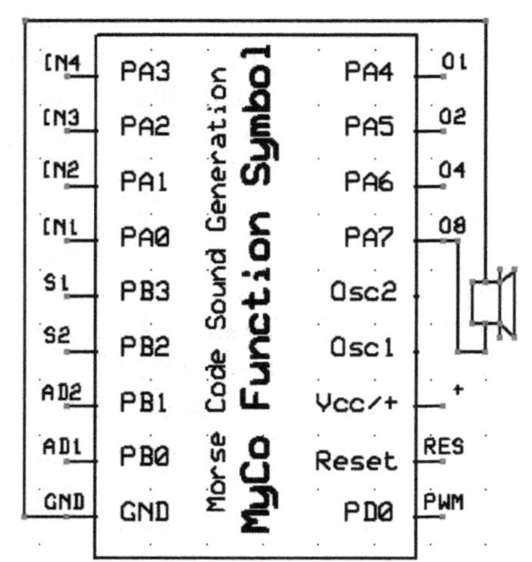

Figure 6.3: Connection of the piezo transducer

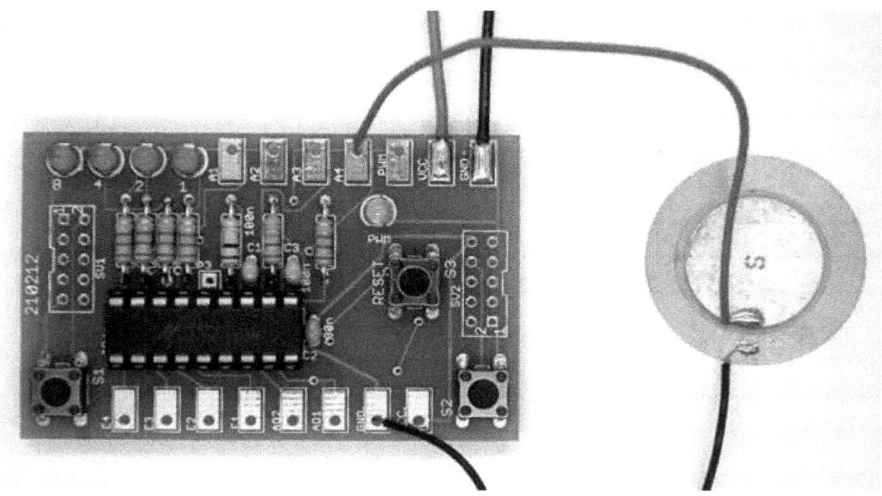

Figure 6.4: Sound output from A4

The pre-programmed subroutine starting at address 50 does not require a page command, as the instruction 85 (set to page 5) had to be used already before the Call. At the same time this subroutine will set the output A1 to High for the duration of the tone. This output signal at A1 can be used to switch an additional external buzzer / light on and off or A1 could even turn a real transmitter on and off.
A long sound will be generated by entering the subroutine at 50; starting the subroutine at 52 will initiate a short sound.

The following program generates in Morse code the letters B and K (the initials the TPS designer Burkhard Kainka). You could call a short program like this an acoustic business card.
Modify the letters to send your own initials.

Morse Code : BK
- long - short - short - short ---long - short - long

Address	Instruction	Data	Comment
00	8	5	AddrHi <=5
01	D	0	Call 50, long
02	2	6	100 ms
03	D	2	Call 52, short

04	2	6	100 ms
05	D	2	Call 52, short
06	2	6	100 ms
07	D	2	Call 52, short
08	2	6	100 ms
09	2	7	200 ms
0A	D	0	Call 50, long
0B	2	6	100 ms
0C	D	2	Call 52, short
0D	2	6	100 ms
0E	D	0	Call 50, long
0F	3	0	End, loop

85 D0 26 D2 26 D2 26 D2 26 27 D0 26 D2 26 D0 30

Listing 6.5: Morse code sound output

Morse Code

A	- —	J	- — — —	S	- - -	1	- — — — —
B	— - - -	K	— - —	T	—	2	- - — — —
C	— - — -	L	- — - -	U	- - —	3	- - - — —
D	— - -	M	— —	V	- - - —	4	- - - - —
E	-	N	— -	W	- — —	5	- - - - -
F	- - — -	O	— — —	X	— - - —	6	— - - - -
G	— — -	P	- — — -	Y	— - — —	7	— — - - -
H	- - - -	Q	— — - —	Z	— — - -	8	— — — - -
I	- -	R	- — -			9	— — — — -
						0	— — — — —

For more about Morse code, see Wikipedia: http://en.wikipedia.org/wiki/Morse_code

6.5 - Start / Stop Timer

Let us build now a Start/Stop switch. What do we need? A switch to start the timer, a delay loop with a predefined resolution, and a switch to stop the timer. S1, S2 and MyCo can do the job easily. As soon as S1 is pushed shortly, a timer with a resolution of 1s starts and counts up. S2 stops the timer (you will have to keep it pushed for more than a second so MyCo understands to stop; this in the way it has been programmed).

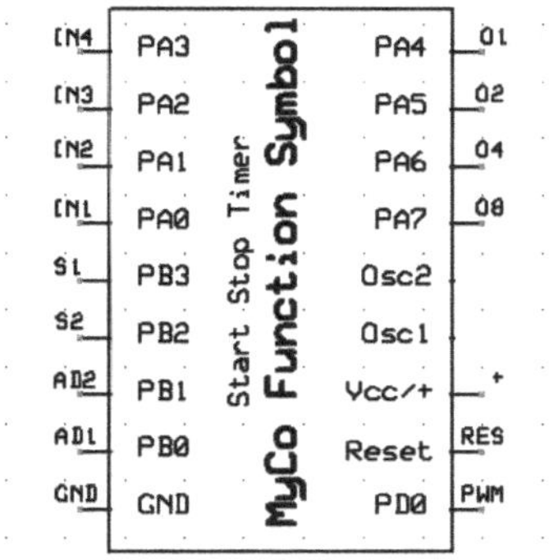

Having finished the timer, you can get it ready for the next measurement by using S2 again; this will reset the counter and the Timer is ready for a new measurement when you push S1 shortly.

Address	Instruction	Data	Comment
00	8	6	Set to Page 6 "Timer Start/Stop"
01	D	0	Call "Wait for S1" on page 6
02	4	0	A <= 0
03	7	1	A <= A + 1
04	5	4	Port <= A
05	2	9	Wait for 1 s
06	C	D	S2 = 0?
07	3	4	Jump to - 4
08	D	8	Call "Wait S2"
09	4	0	A <= 0
0A	5	4	Port <= A
0B	3	B	Jump to - 11 (addr 00)

86 D0 40 71 54 29 CD 34 D8 40 54 3B

Listing 6.6: Stopwatch

The resolution of the timer is set at address 05 and will increment in 1sec steps, so a max time of 16 steps. You can modify this program easily by changing the time delay value at address 05. A change from 29 to 2C will cause it to count in 10sec steps, or with 2F in 1 min steps.

The pre-programmed code contains a timer function which is very similar. The start address is 40, so your code only needs to set the page to go to this subroutine and then go there, as shown in listing 6.7. Look at the complete listing in the Appendix for page 4. There, a waiting instruction of 5ms is used. The effective resolution is about 10ms. Write a short main program with a jump to this address 40 to test this program. With a resolution of 10ms this program can as well be used as a reaction tester.

Address	Instruction	Data	Comment
00	8	4	Set to Page 4
01	9	0	Jump to 40

84 90

Listing 6.7: Main program to start the stopwatch demo program

The next step would be to modify the timing instruction there to 50ms, 500ms or 30sec, to get resolutions of 100ms, 1sec or 1min. Remember, you can always get the factory default programming back easily via FF FF if you did something wrong.

6.6 - Combination Lock

The combination lock presented here must set the PWM output if the user has entered the correct number sequence. The number input is done via the buttons S1 and S2 exactly in the same way as we do the programming.

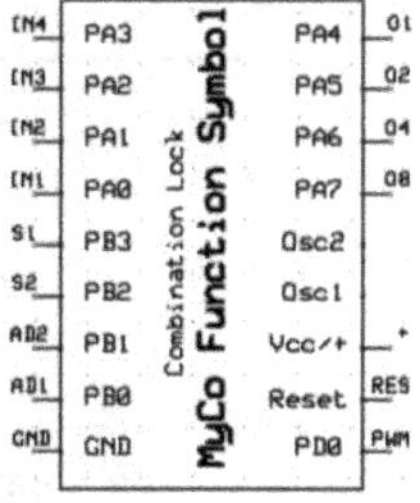

The following program demonstrates the input of a single number using the S1 key. As with the programming process, we reset the internal counter to 0000. Then, with each subsequent S1 press, the internal counter is incremented and the counter status shown on the LEDs.

Pressing S2 takes this contents of the counter as the chosen value, and as one of the secret numbers. Then after all 3 entered, the PWM output is either on as F – correct, or off – wrong number. And the program ends in the endless loop via 30 as often before.

Address	Instruction	Data	Comment
00	C	C	Is S1 = 0?
01	3	1	Jump to - 1
02	4	0	A <= 0
03	5	4	Dout <= A
04	2	3	Wait for 10 ms
05	C	E	Is S1 = 1?
06	3	2	Jump to Addr 04
07	C	F	S2 = 1?
08	3	0	End
09	C	C	Is S1 = 0?
0A	3	3	Jump to Addr 07
0B	7	1	A <= A + 1
0C	2	3	Wait for 10 ms
0D	C	C	Is S1 = 1?
0E	3	1	Jump to Addr 0D
0F	3	C	Jump to Addr 03

CC 31 40 54 23 CE 32 CF 30 CC 33 71 23 CC 31 3C

Listing 6.8: Listing of the combination lock

The number entry program is already provided as a subroutine. You can find it at address 70. Instead of the endless loop in line 08 of listing 6.8 there is a RET instruction in the subroutine coming back to the calling program. It returns with the number counted via S1 in Reg A.

The following combination lock program calls this subroutine located at address 70 three times as call D0 and returns with the number input via S1 in register A. It compares this number in A with the 3 preprogrammed secret numbers that have to be entered not only correctly, but as well in the correct sequence: 3, 5, 2. If all 3 are correct, the PWM output is set to full by setting it to value 15. A wrong number or sequence entered lets the program fall into an infinite loop after each of the 3 comparisons. You can get out only via Reset.

As you can see, the PWM output is used here as an additional digital output with 4 bit resolution, so 0 would be Low and F would be High and the values in between not used in this digital function.
After each entry, the four LEDs showing the number input are cleared quickly to minimize the risk that a casual observer gets any clues of our secret number.

Address	Instruction	Data	Comment
00	8	7	Set to Page 7
01	4	3	A <= 3
02	5	1	B <= A
03	D	0	Call 70
04	C	3	Skip if A=B
05	3	0	End - wrong
06	1	0	LEDs off
07	4	5	A <= 5
08	5	1	B <= A
09	D	0	Call 70
0A	C	3	Skip if A=B
0B	3	0	End - wrong
0C	1	0	LEDs off
0D	4	2	A <= 2
0E	5	1	B <= A
0F	D	0	Call 70
10	C	3	Skip if A=B
11	3	0	End - wrong
12	1	0	LEDs off
13	4	F	A <= 15
14	5	9	PWM <= A
15	3	0	End

87 43 51 D0 C3 30 10 45 51 D0 C3 30 10 42 51 D0 C3 30 10 4F 59 30

Listing 6.9: The combination lock

And as we all know the secret number now, please switch MyCo into programming mode and enter your 3 personal secret numbers for this lock to a number sequence that is only known to you!

Change at address 01 from 3 to your number a
Change at address 07 from 5 to your number b
Change at address 0D from 2 to your number c
And you are safe again.

Now we have unfortunately come to the end of our journey of the first steps in programming. I enjoyed it very much. When I saw that some parts that were missing for me compared to the original in German, I added them in. Knowing roughly what is happening is one thing, but how are these bits/nibbles actually shifted around in this little computer?
This we will see roughly in the next chapter that I have added.

7 - The Inner Workings of MyCo

Having gone through the sample programs and having had a taste, you are probably now ready to understand most the inner workings better:

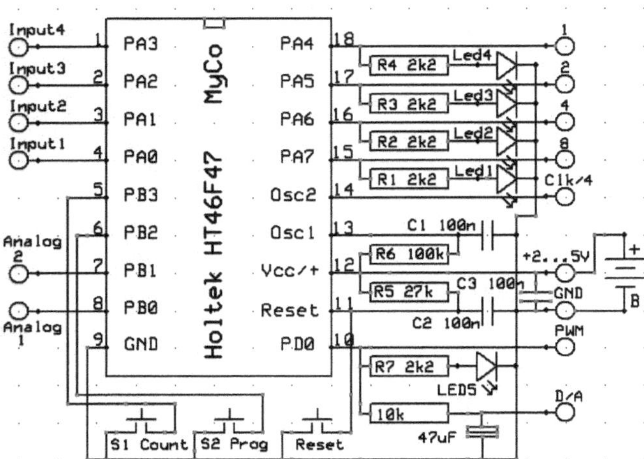

Figure 7.1: The circuit diagram

We have seen this schematic a few times now. We see the 4 inputs, the 2 analog inputs, our 3 switches, the 4 outputs, clock generation with R6 and C1, Reset using R5 and C2, PWM output, and analog output using the RC network. I added the D/A RC to my schematic as it seems right, it is an additional output. Everything ends up at the Holtek Chip HT46F47. But was is actually going on inside?

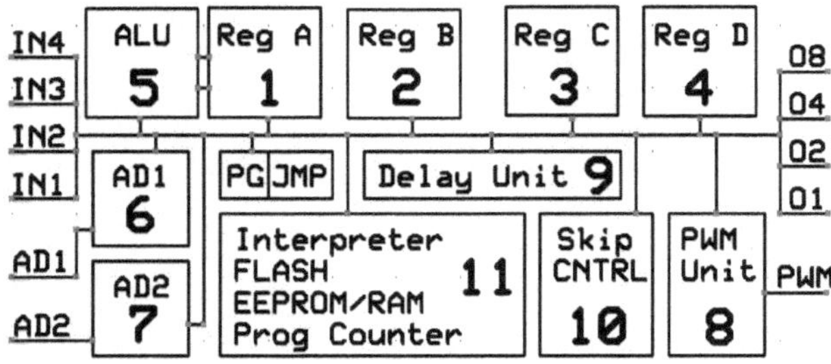

Figure 7.2: The inner functionality as block

Figure 7.3a: The inner functionality all in a row

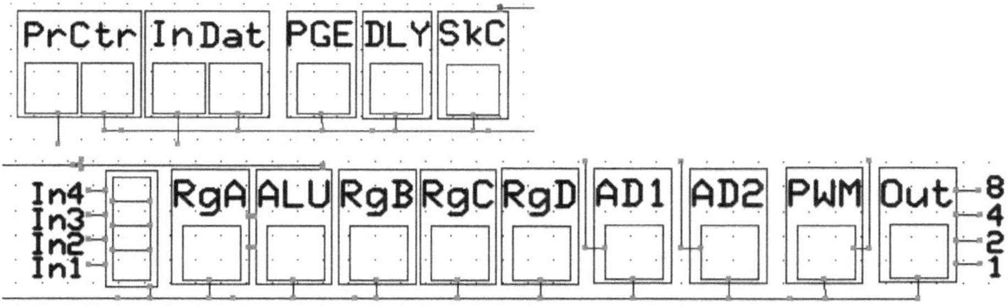

Figure 7.3b: The inner functionality broken into two rows

This inner functionality in a row is for me the best way to understand how MyCo works. First you have the program counter 2 nibbles wide, showing the address of your program.
The next part is your program - Instruction and the Data, one nibble each.
Then the Page counter for jumps to any location within our 128 locations.
Next the delay counter, where the 1ms to 60sec delay is counting down invisibly.
Skip Control gets the input from the ALU and various other sources
and tells the Program Counter either to increment to the next program location if the condition is not met,
or to increment the program counter by 2, skipping over the one instruction.
The next parts are the simulated processor with

> **4 inputs**
> **our main register A,**
> **closely connected to the ALU,**
> **then register B,**
> **C and**
> **D.**
> **AD1 and**
> **AD2** are our two analog inputs with 16 levels of resolution, and
> **PWM** with 16 levels output.
> **Output Register**, 4 bit wide, is the the last block.

In the Appendix there are two programming pages as examples, so you can start programming MyCo even without having one. Just write the program address, instruction, data into the first 2 blocks and add what actually happens internally into the other ones.

Enter 0/L or 1/H into the inputs and the same for the outputs. Values at AD1 and AD inputs show what comes in, and PWM shows what is sent out via a quasi analog output.
Here we have to come to an end. Much more could be said, and might be in the future.
I hope it was interesting to read this eBook and you might be tempted to get a kit for yourself and actually see it working.

Any feedback to this Book please send to epldfpga@aol.com.

We tried to eliminate as many issues, typos, ... as possible.
But we know we are human, so errors are possible, but known ones can be corrected in the next edition, so please keep sending them in.

We can take no responsibility for any results of using this contents.
It is planned mainly for educational use .

8 - Appendix

8.1 - Listing of sample programs

Address	Instruction	Data	Comment
00	6	4	A <= Din
01	5	1	B <= A
02	4	E	A <= 1110
03	8	0	Page 0
04	C	3	A = B?
05	9	8	Jump 08 back
06	8	2	Set page to 2
07	9	5	Jump to 05
08	4	D	A <= 1101
09	8	0	Set to Page 0
0A	C	3	A = B?
0B	9	E	Jump back E addresses
0C	8	2	Set to Page 2
0D	9	A	Jump forward 2A, AD/PWM
0E	4	B	A <= 1011
0F	8	1	Set to Page 1

64 51 4E 80 C3 98 82 95 4D 80 C3 9E 82 9A 4B 81

Page 0 of the EEPROM, and starting from 0 after Reset: selection and start of example programs

Address	Instruction	Data	Comment
10	C	3	A = B?
11	9	4	Jump 4 forward
12	8	3	Set to Page 3
13	9	0	Jump to 30, "Random"
14	4	7	A <= 0111
15	8	1	Set to Page1
16	C	3	Is A =B?
17	9	A	Jump A forward
18	8	3	Set to Page 3
19	9	4	Jump 4 forward, "Stop S1"
1A	4	3	A <= 0011
1B	8	2	Set to 2
1C	C	3	Is A =B?
1D	9	0	Jump by0 "LED blink"
1E	8	4	Set to Page 4
1F	9	0	Jump forward 0 "Stop S1/S2"

C3 94 83 90 47 81 C3 9A 83 94 43 82 C3 90 84 90

Page 1: Select and run the example programs

Address	Instruction	Data	Comment
20	1	1	Output 0001 "2 LED Blink"
21	2	8	Wait for 500 ms
22	1	8	Output 1000
23	2	8	Wait for 500 ms
24	3	4	Jump 4 back 4
25	7	1	A <= A + 1 "Count"
26	5	4	Port <= A
27	5	9	PWM <= A
28	2	6	Wait for100 ms
29	3	4	Jump - 4
2A	6	9	A <= AD1 "AD/PWM"
2B	5	4	Port <= A
2C	5	9	PWM <= A
2D	2	6	Wait for 100 ms
2E	3	4	Jump by - 4
2F	F	F	-

11 28 18 28 34 71 54 59 26 34 69 54 59 26 34 FF

Page 2: Example programs: alternate flashing, counting, AD / PWM

Address	Instruction	Data	Comment
30	5	4	Port <= A "Random"
31	C	E	S1 <= 1?
32	7	1	A <= A + 1
33	3	3	Jump - 3
34	2	2	Wait for 5 ms "Stop on S1"
35	C	C	Is S1 = 0?
36	3	2	Jump by -2
37	4	0	A <= 0
38	2	2	Wait for 5 ms
39	7	1	A <= A + 1
3A	5	4	Port <= A
2B	C	E	S1 = 1?
3C	3	4	Jump by - 4
3D	3	9	Jump by - 9
3E	F	F	-
3F	F	F	-

54 CE 71 33 22 CC 32 40 22 71 54 CE 34 39 FF FF

Page 3: Example programs: random number, stopwatch S1

Address	Instruction	Data	Comment
40	8	6	Set to Page 6 "Start/Stop"
41	D	0	Call "Wait S1"
42	4	0	A <= 0
43	7	1	A <= A + 1
44	5	4	Port <= A
45	2	3	Wait for10 ms
46	C	D	Is S2 = 0?
47	3	4	Jump by - 4
48	D	8	Call "Wait for S2"
49	4	0	A <= 0
4A	5	4	Port <= A
4B	3	B	Jump by - 11
4C	F	F	-
4D	F	F	-
4E	F	F	-
4F	F	F	-

86 D0 40 71 54 23 CD 34 D8 40 54 3B FF FF FF FF

Page 4: Example program stop watch start / stop

Address	Instruction	Data	Comment
50	4	F	A<=15 "Sound long"
51	9	3	Jump to Addr 03
52	4	5	A<=5 "Sound short"
53	5	3	D<=A "Sound variable"
54	1	9	A4 <= 1
55	1	1	A4 <= 0
56	2	1	2 ms delay
57	1	9	A4 <= 1
58	1	1	A4 <= 0
59	2	1	2 ms
5A	1	9	A4 <= 1
5B	1	1	A4 <= 0
5C	2	0	delay 1 ms
5D	B	4	D times 04
5E	1	0	Dout <=0
5F	E	0	Return

4F 93 45 53 19 11 21 19 11 21 19 11 20 B4 10 E0

Page 5: Subroutine sound output

Address	Instruction	Data	Comment
60	2	3	Wait 10 ms "Wait S1"
61	C	E	S1 = 1?
62	3	2	Jump to - 2
63	2	3	Wait for 10 ms
64	C	C	S1 = 0?
65	3	1	Jump to - 1
66	E	0	Return
67	F	F	-
68	2	3	Wait for 10 ms "Wait S2"
69	C	F	S2 = 1?
6A	3	2	Jump to - 2
6B	2	3	Wait for 10 ms
6C	C	D	S2 = 0?
6D	3	1	Jump to - 1
6E	E	0	Return
6F	F	F	-

23 CE 32 23 CC 31 E0 FF 23 CF 32 23 CD 31 E0 FF

Page 6: Subroutines waiting for S1 and for S2

Address	Instruction	Data	Comment
70	C	C	S1 = 0? "Switch Input"
71	3	1	Jump to - 1
72	4	0	A = 0
73	5	4	Port = A
74	2	3	Wait for 10 ms
75	C	E	S1 = 1?
76	3	2	Jump to - 2
77	C	F	S2 = 1?
78	E	0	Return
79	C	C	S1 = 0?
7A	3	3	Jump to - 3
7B	7	1	A = A + 1
7C	2	3	Wait for 10 ms
7D	C	C	S1 = 1?
7E	3	1	Jump to - 1
7F	3	C	Jump to - 12

CC 31 40 54 23 CE 32 CF E0 CC 33 71 23 CC 31 3C

Page 7: Subroutine switch input

8.2 - Instruction Table

	1	2	3	4	5	6	7	8	9	A	B	C	D	E
	to Port	Wait	Jump back	A<= ...	... <=A	A<= ...	A<= ...	Set Page	Jump (Page)	C*	D*	Skip if ...	Call	Ret
0	0	1 ms	0	0				0	0	0	0		0	
1	1	2 ms	1	1	B<=A	A<= B	A<=A+1	1	1	1	1	A>B	1	
2	2	5 ms	2	2	C<=A	A<=C	A<=A–1	2	2	2	2	A<B	2	
3	3	10	3	3	D<=A	A<=D	A<=A+B	3	3	3	3	A=B	3	
4	4	20	4	4	Dout<=A	A<=Din	A<=A–B	4	4	4	4	Din.0=1	4	
5	5	50	5	5	A.0	A<=Din.0	A<= A*B	5	5	5	5	Din.1=1	5	
6	6	100	6	6	A.0	A<=Din.1	A<=A/B	6	6	6	6	Din.2=1	6	
7	7	200	7	7	A.0	A<=Din.2	B	7	7	7	7	Din.3=1	7	
8	8	500	8	8	A.0	A<=Din.3	A<=A Or B		8	8	8	Din.0=0	8	
9	9	1 s	9	9	PWM<=A	A<=AD1	A<= A Xor		9	9	9	Din.1=0	9	
A	10	2 s	10	10		A<=AD2	A<=Not A		A	A	A	Din.2=0	A	
B	11	5 s	11	11					B	B	B	Din.3=0	B	
C	12	10 s	12	12					C	C	C	S1=0	C	
D	13	20 s	13	13					D	D	D	S2=0	D	
E	14	30 s	14	14					E	E	E	S1=1	E	
F	15	60 s	15	15					F	F	F	S2=1	F	

8.3 - Programming Model A

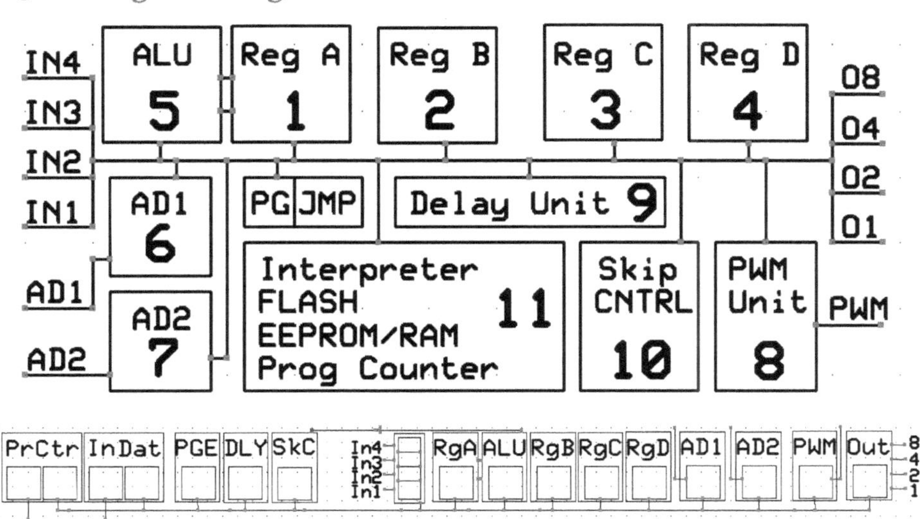

Programming Model B, all in one row

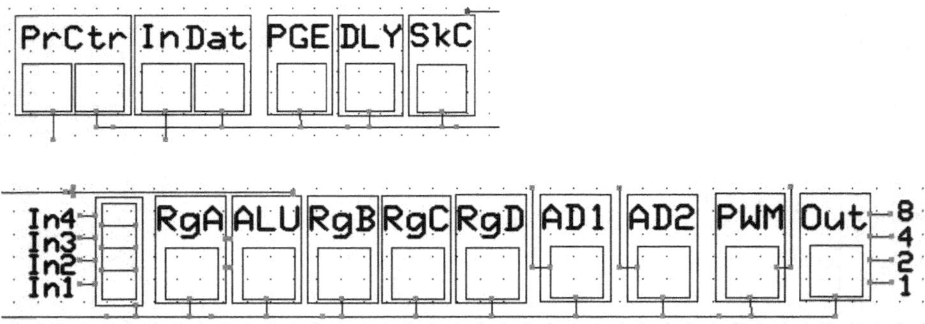

Programming model C, split up

8.4 - MyCo Circuit Diagram

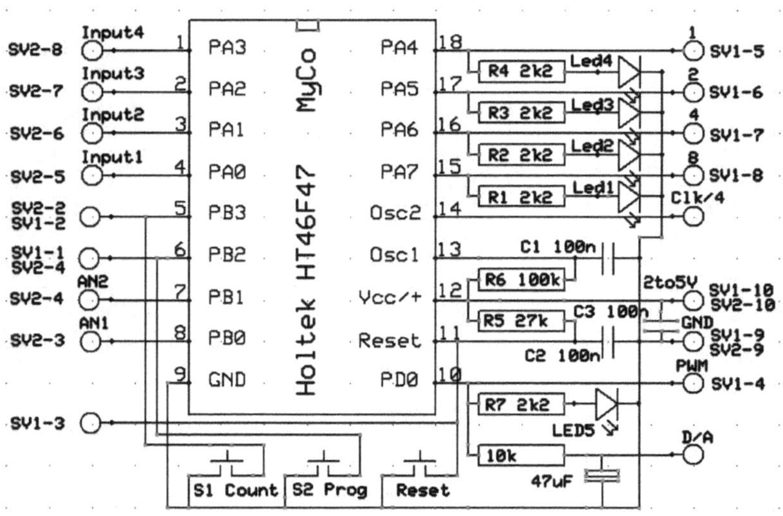

8.5 - MyCo Function Symbol

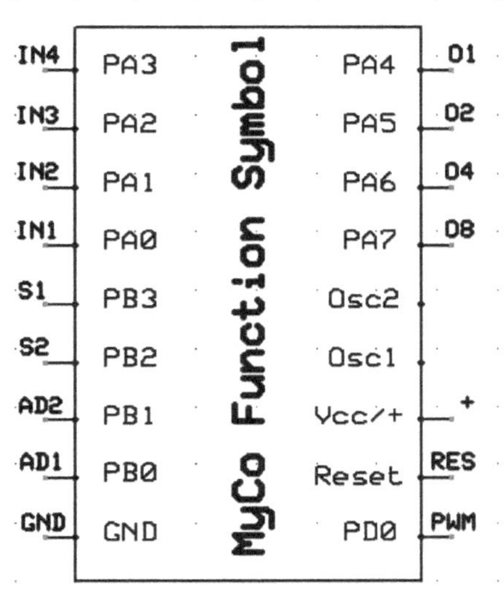

8.6 - PCB top view with all components

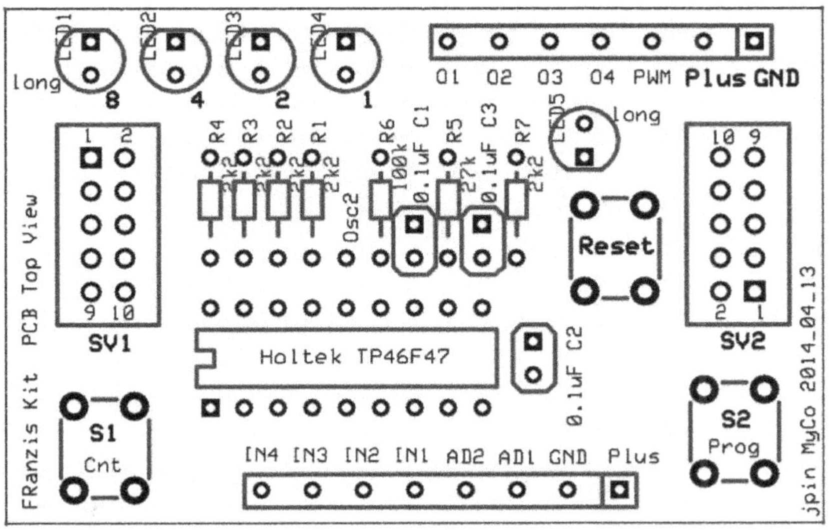

8.7 – Header Connectors

S2	1	2	S1
Reset	3	4	PWM
A1	5	6	A2
A3	7	8	A4
GND	9	10	VCC

8.7a - Header connector SV1same way on the board

S2	1	2	S1
AD1	3	4	AD2
E1	5	6	E2
E3	7	8	E4
GND	9	10	VCC

8.7b - Header connector SV2, turned 180 degrees on the board
if populated, use angled version

I used a straight header on SV2 as I had it available, but found it was difficult to use the Reset then. As help and solution I shortened them, as I only wanted to use them for soldering. It is a good idea to pre-solder the rest, but as a silly there was a solder bridge. Murphy's law states it is always to the worst combination – and it was, the nearly invisible bridge shortcircuiting 9 and 10 on SV2, so no function as of this short circuit between plus and minus of the battery, and the battery started to heat up. Shortly afterwards I saw the problem, removed the short, problem solved, back to normal.

8.8 - Binary, Decimal and Hexadecimal Table

„8“	„4“	„2“	„1“	Decimal	Hexadecimal
0	0	0	0	0	0
0	0	0	1	1	1
0	0	1	0	2	2
0	0	1	1	3	3
0	1	0	0	4	4
0	1	0	1	5	5
0	1	1	0	6	6
0	1	1	1	7	7
1	0	0	0	8	8
1	0	0	1	9	9
1	0	1	0	10	A
1	0	1	1	11	B
1	1	0	0	12	C
1	1	0	1	13	D
1	1	1	0	14	E
1	1	1	1	15	F

8.9 - Block diagram of the processor, (source Holtek)

Link to the Holtek processor used here

http://www.holtek.com/english/docum/uc/46f4xe.htm

And the data sheet http://www.holtek.com/pdf/uc/46f4xev140.pdf

Block Diagram

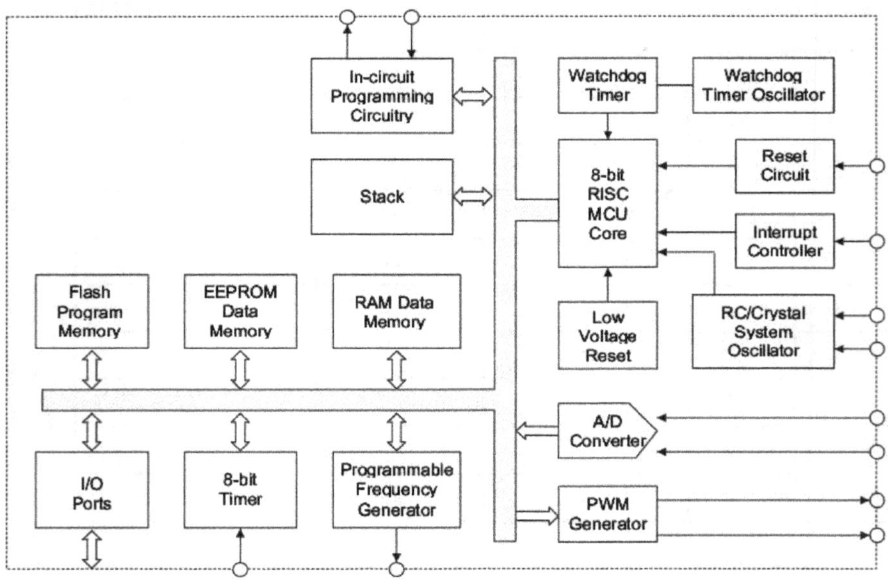

8.10 - My Maplin test breadboard

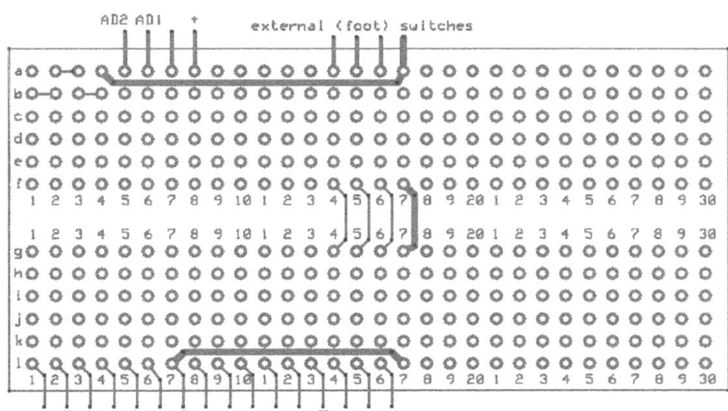

I bought a DIL switch to change the input signals E1 to E4 easily, with the 8 as it turned out, AN1, AN2, plus and ground can be switched as well.
Take a cut off LED wire from the build and solder it onto the black wire of the piezo, helps to fix it on to the breadboard.
A suitable plastic box is available from Maplin. It keeps the board and the battery case safe.

8.11 - Resistor Color Code (if no Internet within reach)

Colour	1st Band	2nd Band	3rd band	Multiplier	Tolerance
Black	0	0	0	1 Ohm	±1%
Brown	1	1	1	10 Ohm	±2%
Red	2	2	2	100 Ohm	
Orange	3	3	3	1kOhm	
Yellow	4	4	4	10kOhm	
Green	5	5	5	100kOhm	±0.5 %
Blue	6	6	6	1 MOhm	± 0.25%
Violet	7	7	7	10 MOhm	± 0.1%
Grey	8	8	8		±0.0.5%
White	9	9	9		
Gold				0.1 Ohm	±5%
Silver				0.01 Ohm	±10%

8.12 - Toolbox to draw the flow diagrams:

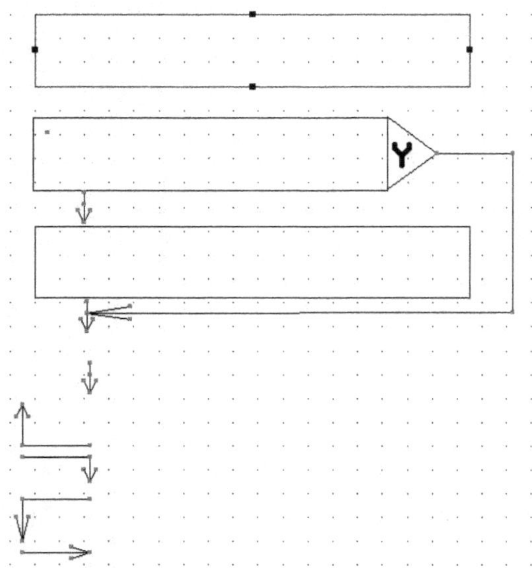

Square box to describe what the Instruction does,

Square Box with Exit Y:

if condition NO just continue,
if condition met YES skip over next Instruction

Arrow to next Instruction

Jump back
Come back in

Jump forward
Get back in line,

and next would be the small arrow down into the next block

8.13 - Interfacing MyCo to the PC to download programs

If you are one of the lucky ones that owns an old PC with Serial or Parallel Port - not just USB,
you can actually drive and control MyCo using Abacom Digital-Profilab 4.0.

I own it for many years now, and can only recommend it.

The best option is the Parallel Interface, as there are sufficient pins to control and read what MyCo needs.

The Serial Port will give you just enough "pins" so you can control MyCo,
but you need to do the level shifting, as the serial lines are up to plus and minus 15 V.
3 lines for wired OR of the 3 switches
4 lines Input - see the status of the LEDs
Exactly what is needed. Well, you lose the PWM as there is no line left

You can download a free version to try it out at www.abacom-online.de
Trial versions do not allow saving of your program.

You can even use more of the modules of Profilab, define code, store it on the PC and send the code down to MyCo, simulating the programming cycle.

From the Profilab documentation:

COM port (direct port access)

Included in version:
DMM-ProfiLab: Yes Digital-ProfiLab: Yes ProfiLab-Expert: Yes

The COM port may be used to control external hardware as well. But level shifting is needed.
The following pins are useable at the serial COM port:

4 digital inputs (CTS, DSR, RI, DCD) read in the outputs via transistor interface

3 digital outputs (DTR, RTS, TxD) control MyCo via 3 switches connected via level shifters.

The pin assignment of the COM port depends on the connector (9 pins or 25 pins):

Connector with 25 pins:

CTS	**Pin 5**
DSR	**Pin 6**
RI	**Pin 22**
DCD	**Pin 8**

DTR	**Pin 20**
RTS	**Pin 4**
TxD	**Pin 2**

Connector with 9 pins:

CTS	**Pin 8**
DSR	**Pin 6**
RI	**Pin 9**
DCD	**Pin 1**

DTR	**Pin 4**
RTS	**Pin 7**
TxD	**Pin 3**

Please pay attention to the voltage levels of the Serial COM port: Low level is indicated by negative voltage between −3V and −15V, while voltages from +3V to +15V represent High level.

Use for example resistors and 3 transistors in parallel to the 3 switches to control via the PC, and protect the PC inputs in a similar way; unfortunately there was no time left to get it all ready before publishing, but there might be a compiled version and more data for you to download to have a remotely controlled MyCo and all of the programs stored on PC.

For PCs with USB interface only: there are USB to Serial, USB to Parallel modules available to achieve a similar functionality.

And for easy access and to use the information in this eBook even without the hardware,
the three main parts again: Circuit Diagram with external components connected, Instruction Table, Programming Pages:

8.14a - Circuit diagram plus external parts

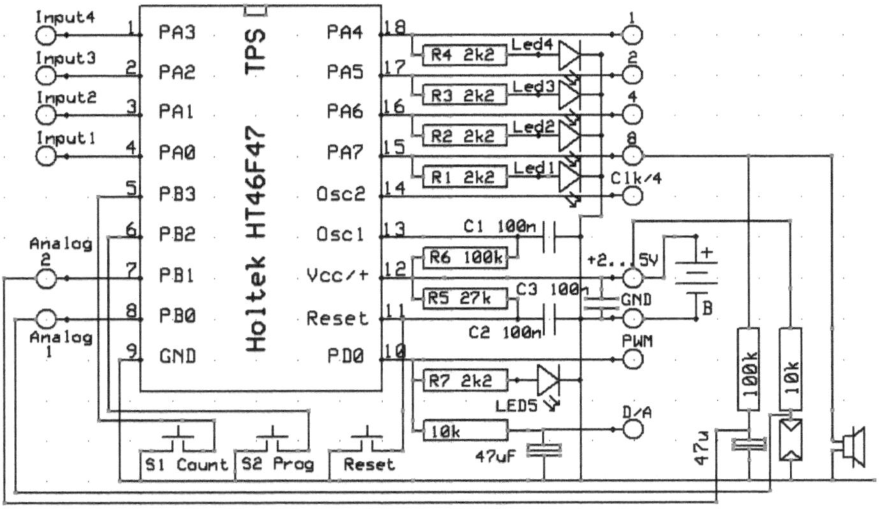

8.14b - Instruction Table

	1	2	3	4	5	6	7	8	9	A	B	C	D	E
	to Port	Wait	Jump back	A<= ...	... <=A	A<= ...	A<= ...	Set Page	Jump (Page)	C*	D*	Skip if ...	Call	Ret
0	0	1 ms	0	0				0	0	0	0		0	
1	1	2 ms	1	1	B<=A	A<= B	A<=A+1	1	1	1	1	A>B	1	
2	2	5 ms	2	2	C<=A	A<=C	A<=A–1	2	2	2	2	A<B	2	
3	3	10	3	3	D<=A	A<=D	A<=A+B	3	3	3	3	A=B	3	
4	4	20	4	4	Dout<=A	A<=Din	A<=A–B	4	4	4	4	Din.0=1	4	
5	5	50	5	5	A.0	A<=Din.0	A<= A*B	5	5	5	5	Din.1=1	5	
6	6	100	6	6	A.0	A<=Din.1	A<=A/B	6	6	6	6	Din.2=1	6	
7	7	200	7	7	A.0	A<=Din.2	B	7	7	7	7	Din.3=1	7	
8	8	500	8	8	A.0	A<=Din.3	A<=A Or B		8	8	8	Din.0=0	8	
9	9	1 s	9	9	PWM<=A	A<=AD1	A<= A Xor		9	9	9	Din.1=0	9	
A	10	2 s	10	10		A<=AD2	A<=Not A		A	A	A	Din.2=0	A	
B	11	5 s	11	11					B	B	B	Din.3=0	B	
C	12	10 s	12	12					C	C	C	S1=0	C	
D	13	20 s	13	13					D	D	D	S2=0	D	
E	14	30 s	14	14					E	E	E	S1=1	E	
F	15	60 s	15	15					F	F	F	S2=1	F	

8.15 - Programming Pages

ProCtr InsDat Pg Dly Skp In4 In3 In2 In1 RgA ALU RgB RgC RgD AD1 AD1 PWM OUT 8 4 2 1

ProCtr InsDat Pg Dly Skp In4 In3 In2 In1 RgA ALU RgB RgC RgD AD1 AD1 PWM OUT 8 4 2 1

ProCtr InsDat Pg Dly Skp In4 In3 In2 In1 RgA ALU RgB RgC RgD AD1 AD1 PWM OUT 8 4 2 1

ProCtr InsDat Pg Dly Skp In4 In3 In2 In1 RgA ALU RgB RgC RgD AD1 AD1 PWM OUT 8 4 2 1

ProCtr InsDat Pg Dly Skp In4 In3 In2 In1 RgA ALU RgB RgC RgD AD1 AD1 PWM OUT 8 4 2 1

ProCtr InsDat Pg Dly Skp In4 In3 In2 In1 RgA ALU RgB RgC RgD AD1 AD1 PWM OUT 8 4 2 1

ProCtr InsDat Pg Dly Skp In4 In3 In2 In1 RgA ALU RgB RgC RgD AD1 AD1 PWM OUT 8 4 2 1

ProCtr InsDat Pg Dly Skp In4 In3 In2 In1 RgA ALU RgB RgC RgD AD1 AD1 PWM OUT 8 4 2 1

ProCtr InsDat Pg Dly Skp In4 In3 In2 In1 RgA ALU RgB RgC RgD AD1 AD1 PWM OUT 8 4 2 1

ProCtr InsDat Pg Dly Skp In4 In3 In2 In1 RgA ALU RgB RgC RgD AD1 AD1 PWM OUT 8 4 2 1

ProCtr InsDat Pg Dly Skp In4 In3 In2 In1 RgA ALU RgB RgC RgD AD1 AD1 PWM OUT 8 4 2 1

ProCtr InsDat Pg Dly Skp In4 In3 In2 In1 RgA ALU RgB RgC RgD AD1 AD1 PWM OUT 8 4 2 1

ProCtr InsDat Pg Dly Skp In4 In3 In2 In1 RgA ALU RgB RgC RgD AD1 AD1 PWM OUT 8 4 2 1

ProCtr InsDat Pg Dly Skp In4 In3 In2 In1 RgA ALU RgB RgC RgD AD1 AD1 PWM OUT 8 4 2 1

ProCtr InsDat Pg Dly Skp In4 In3 In2 In1 RgA ALU RgB RgC RgD AD1 AD1 PWM OUT 8 4 2 1

ProCtr InsDat Pg Dly Skp In4 In3 In2 In1 RgA ALU RgB RgC RgD AD1 AD1 PWM OUT 8 4 2 1

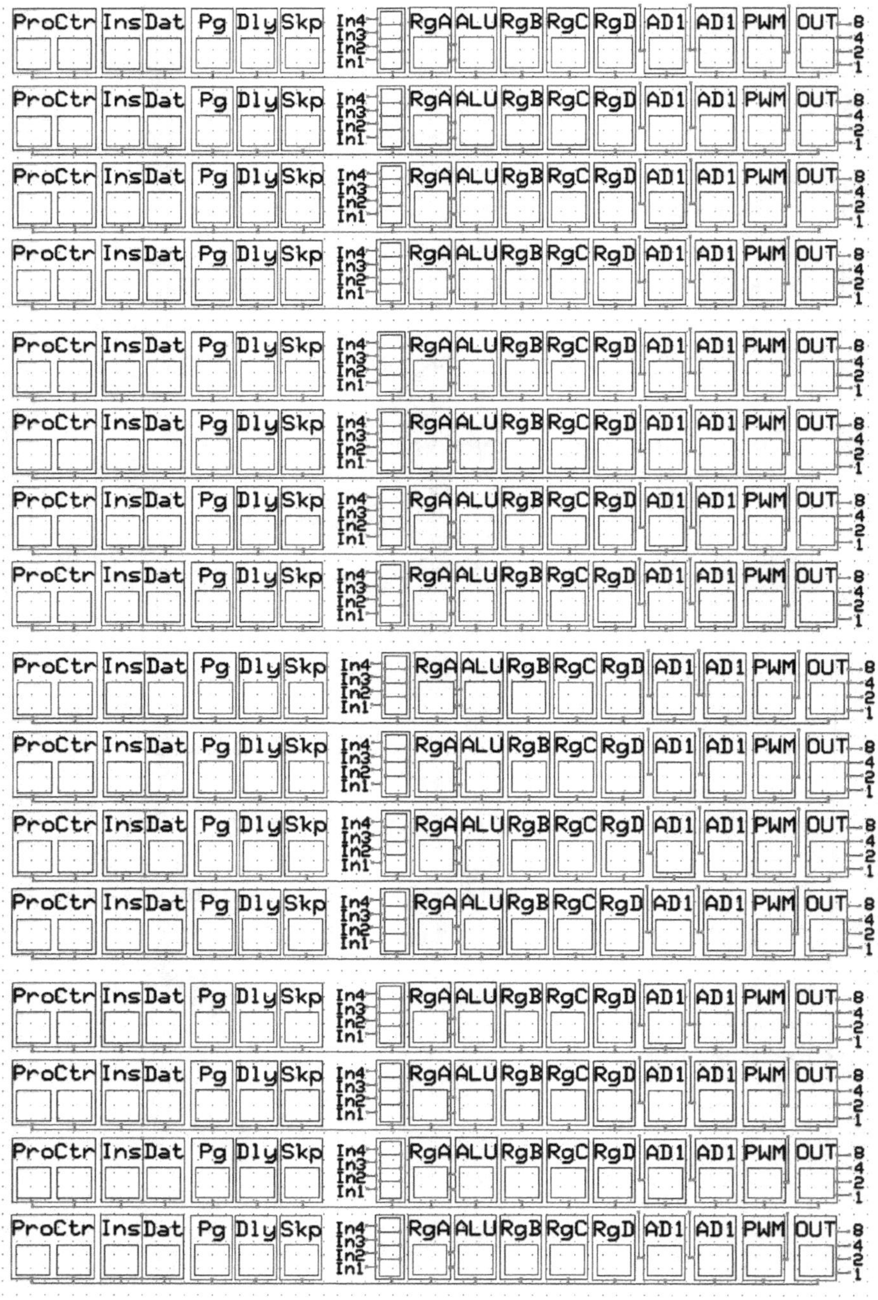

ProCtr Ins Dat Pg Dly Skp In4 In3 In2 In1 RgA ALU RgB RgC RgD AD1 AD1 PWM OUT 8 4 2 1

ProCtr Ins Dat Pg Dly Skp In4 In3 In2 In1 RgA ALU RgB RgC RgD AD1 AD1 PWM OUT 8 4 2 1

ProCtr Ins Dat Pg Dly Skp In4 In3 In2 In1 RgA ALU RgB RgC RgD AD1 AD1 PWM OUT 8 4 2 1

ProCtr Ins Dat Pg Dly Skp In4 In3 In2 In1 RgA ALU RgB RgC RgD AD1 AD1 PWM OUT 8 4 2 1

ProCtr Ins Dat Pg Dly Skp In4 In3 In2 In1 RgA ALU RgB RgC RgD AD1 AD1 PWM OUT 8 4 2 1

ProCtr Ins Dat Pg Dly Skp In4 In3 In2 In1 RgA ALU RgB RgC RgD AD1 AD1 PWM OUT 8 4 2 1

ProCtr Ins Dat Pg Dly Skp In4 In3 In2 In1 RgA ALU RgB RgC RgD AD1 AD1 PWM OUT 8 4 2 1

ProCtr Ins Dat Pg Dly Skp In4 In3 In2 In1 RgA ALU RgB RgC RgD AD1 AD1 PWM OUT 8 4 2 1

ProCtr Ins Dat Pg Dly Skp In4 In3 In2 In1 RgA ALU RgB RgC RgD AD1 AD1 PWM OUT 8 4 2 1

ProCtr Ins Dat Pg Dly Skp In4 In3 In2 In1 RgA ALU RgB RgC RgD AD1 AD1 PWM OUT 8 4 2 1

ProCtr Ins Dat Pg Dly Skp In4 In3 In2 In1 RgA ALU RgB RgC RgD AD1 AD1 PWM OUT 8 4 2 1

ProCtr Ins Dat Pg Dly Skp In4 In3 In2 In1 RgA ALU RgB RgC RgD AD1 AD1 PWM OUT 8 4 2 1

ProCtr Ins Dat Pg Dly Skp In4 In3 In2 In1 RgA ALU RgB RgC RgD AD1 AD1 PWM OUT 8 4 2 1

ProCtr Ins Dat Pg Dly Skp In4 In3 In2 In1 RgA ALU RgB RgC RgD AD1 AD1 PWM OUT 8 4 2 1

ProCtr Ins Dat Pg Dly Skp In4 In3 In2 In1 RgA ALU RgB RgC RgD AD1 AD1 PWM OUT 8 4 2 1

ProCtr Ins Dat Pg Dly Skp In4 In3 In2 In1 RgA ALU RgB RgC RgD AD1 AD1 PWM OUT 8 4 2 1

8.16 - Links

A link to Burkhard Kainka's website, where it all started:
http://www.elektronik-labor.de/Projekte/TPS5.html

If you want more pre-programmed MyCo chips, search for TPS in the search box, top left at http://www.ak-modul-bus.de/cgi-bin/iboshop.cgi?search,0

Published as eBook as first version: MyCo_ebook_v17_2014_06_19

This is probably one of the few computers that you can program "handsfree". We tried quickly a version where we used 3 foot switches in parallel to the existing S1, S2 and Reset – and it worked.
Needs getting used to though.

Just in time some other ways to build MyCo:

Version 1: A smaller version, wired underneath with copper wire

Version 2: A "Dremel" Version, no holes, ready to be integrated into a project. Using an engraving tool to make the PCB on the top side.

Thanks to Ralf Lieb for the idea and the video to prove it works.

There will be versions with code for other microcontrollers to add to this Holtek version; we are aiming for Atmel, Microchip and TI MSP430 processors for now.

8.17 - MSP430G2553 as base board and the shield with the IO

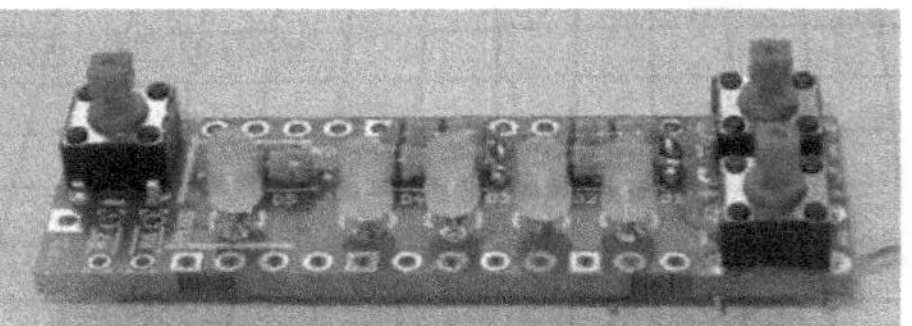

Wires connected to base board   Base board / shield connected to PC

Both boards and 2032 battery   or base board with 2xAAA batteries

Both in TicTac Box used for ExMark MicroBox project and Forth–

Thanks for reading our eBook, and we hope you had some fun and might actually be tempted to spend the little money to buy a kit and see it working. We might do an additional eBook later if enough new material is available.
So we might meet again.

October 2015 - Juergen Pintaske - ExMark   End of version 1 ####

9 - Additional Chapter ARDUINO

Wilfried Klaas had done a Simulator at the time of writing of the eBook. But the code could not be easily transfered to MyCo.

Times have changed and there are 2 platforms more for the Maker community:

Raspberry Pi **Arduino with TPS Interface**

This Simulator on PC can be switched to different Hardware implementations:

TPS Holtek – the original
TPS ATMega8
Willie's TPS ATTINY84
Willie's TPS ARDUINO

Adapting this documentation here to these options will take some time. The easier way is to give people immediate access and to include some material into this book and add the relevant links, where the data can be more easuily extended.

One of these targets is Arduino now, and as there are many of these systems out there, people can easily try out this TPS.

Just as explanation. I tried to translate TPS at the time, but no option I found seemed to reflect what it is.

For this reason I came up with the name MyCo – My Computer. Small and independent.

9.1 - The Simulator and the Row of Buttons

```
|-- EXIT the program
|  |-- CREATE a NEW program ( Control+N )
|  |  |-- OPEN a file ( Control+O )
|  |  |  |-- SAVE the actual program ( Control + S )
|  |  |  |  |-- ADD a new line to the program
|  |  |  |  |  |-- DELETE the actual line
|  |  |  |  |  |  |-- SHOW the actual programming file
|  |  |  |  |  |  |  |-- UPLOAD the program to the target ( Control+U )
|  |  |  |  |  |  |  |  |-- CREATE a HEX file
|  |  |  |  |  |  |  |  |  |-- EXECUTE a single instruction ( F5 )
|  |  |  |  |  |  |  |  |  |  |-- Execute the next step ( F8 )
|  |  |  |  |  |  |  |  |  |  |  |-- STOP the debug program execution ( F6 )
|  |  |  |  |  |  |  |  |  |  |  |  |-- START / STOP program execution ( F9)
|  |  |  |  |  |  |  |  |  |  |  |  |  |-SELECT target Holtek-Mega8-TINY84-Arduino
```

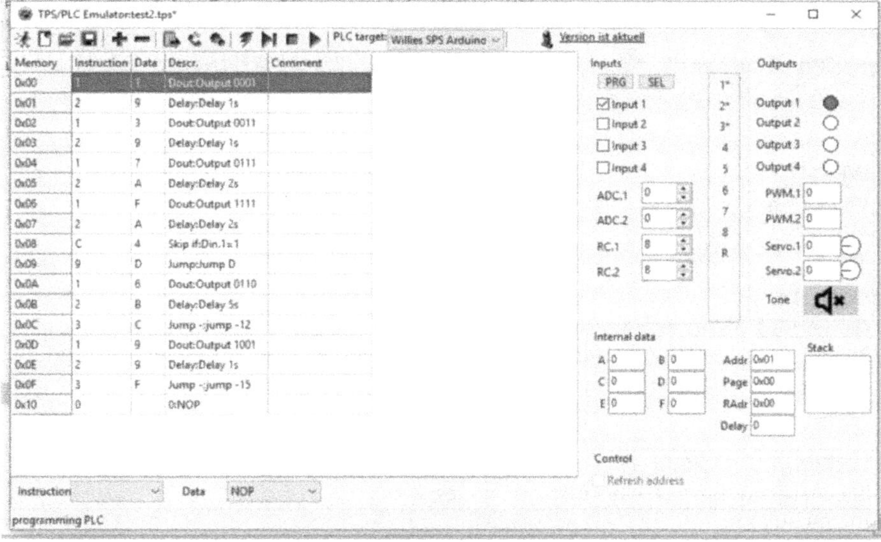

Memory: Showing the memory locations where the instructions are stored

Instruction: Instruction to be executed at the memory execution

Data: Data related to the instruction

Description: Automatically added description

Comment: Own comment to be added

Instruction: Instruction to be inserted into the current memory location

Data: Then open Data and select related number or function

9.2 - The Function Window - on the right hand side

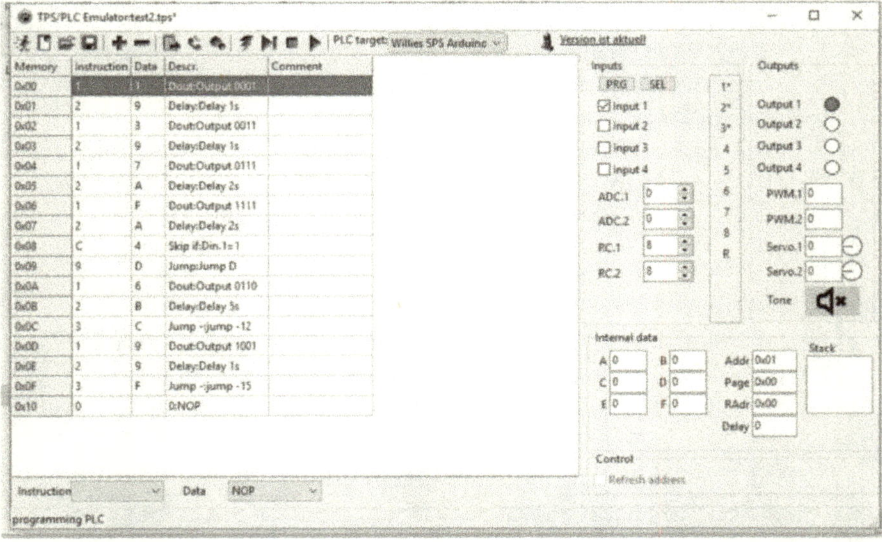

PRG / Program **SEL** / Select

INPUTS:

Input 1 – 4	The four inputs to be set by mouse click
ADC 1, 2	Two simulated analog inputs – input a number between 0 ... 255
RC1, 2	Two simulated RC servo outputs – input a number between 0 ... 255

OUTPUTS:

Output 1 – 4	The four output bits sent by the PLC – Programmable Logic Controller
PWM 1, 2	Pulse Width Modulated outputs, an ON / OFF rectangular output signal
Servo 1, 2	RC servo outputs, simulating the angle by showing a number plus icon
Tone:	A sound to be output – to be added later

INTERNAL DATA of this PLC:

The inputs are fed via the instructions into registers
RA, RB, RC, RD, (RE, RF) and processed

Addr	The current memory location addressed
Page	Each memory block page consists of 16 locations, the page display changes accordingly And JUMPs will setting up a PAGE number if different
Radr	**RETURN ADDRESS** – if subroutine is called, return address is shown here

DELAY	Showing time is a delay instruction is executed
(SKIP	If a skip decision is executed, 1 indicates jump over next instruction **) tbd**

9.3 - Instruction Table

Instruction Set shaded in yellow aextensions of ArduinoSPS/ATTiny84 version.

	0	1	2	3	4	5	6	7
	n.n.	Port	Delay	Jump back rel	A=	„=A“	A=	A= Options
0	NOP	off	1ms	0	0	A<->B		
1		1	2ms	1	1	B=A	A=B	A=A + 1
2		2	5ms	2	2	C=A	A=C	A=A - 1
3		3	10ms	3	3	D=A	A=D	A=A + B
4		4	20ms	4	4	Dout=A	Din	A=A - B
5		5	50ms	5	5	Dout.0=A.0	Din.0	A=A * B
6		6	100ms	6	6	Dout.1=A.0	Din.1	A=A / B
7		7	200ms	7	7	Dout.2=A.0	Din.2	A=A and B
8		8	500ms	8	8	Dout.3=A.0	Din.3	A=A or B
9		9	1s	9	9	PWM.0=A	ADC.0	A=A xor B
a		10	2s	10	10	PWM.1=A	ADC.1	A= not A
b		11	5s	11	11	Servo.0=A	RCin.0	A= A % B (Rem.)
c		12	10s	12	12	Servo.1=A	RCin.1	A= A + 16 * B
d		13	20s	13	13	E=A	A=E	A= B - A
e		14	30s	14	14	F=A	A=F	
f		15	60s	15	15	Push A	Pop A	

8	9	a	b	c	d	e	f
Page	Jump absolute	C*	D*	Skip if	Call # + (16* Page)	Callsub /Ret	Byte Instr.
0	0	0	0	A=0	0	ret	A=ADC.0
1	1	1	1	A>B	1	Call 1	A=ADC.1
2	2	2	2	A<B	2	2	A=RCin.0
3	3	3	3	A=B	3	3	A=RCin.1
4	4	4	4	Din.0=1	4	4	PWM.0=A
5	5	5	5	Din.1=1	5	5	PWM.1=A
6	6	6	6	Din.2=1	6	6	Servo.0=A
7	7	7	7	Din.3=1	7		Servo.1=A
8	8	8	8	Din.0=0	8	Def 1	
9	9	9	9	Din.1=0	9	2	
10	10	10	10	Din.2=0	10	3	
11	11	11	11	Din.3=0	11	4	
12	12	12	12	S_PRG=0	12	5	
13	13	13	13	S_SEL=0	13	6	
14	14	14	14	S_PRG=1	14		
15	15	15	15	S_SEL=1	15	restart	PrgEnd

9.4 - TPS / SPS Emulator

http://wkla.no-ip.biz/ArduinoWiki/doku.php?id=arduino:arduinosps:spsemu

Switch top left to English if needed. The text here is copied from Willie's website.

For the TPS PLC (and my extensions) I once wrote an emulator as a fun project.
Here the result.

The complete project is programmed in Lazarus (Freepascal).

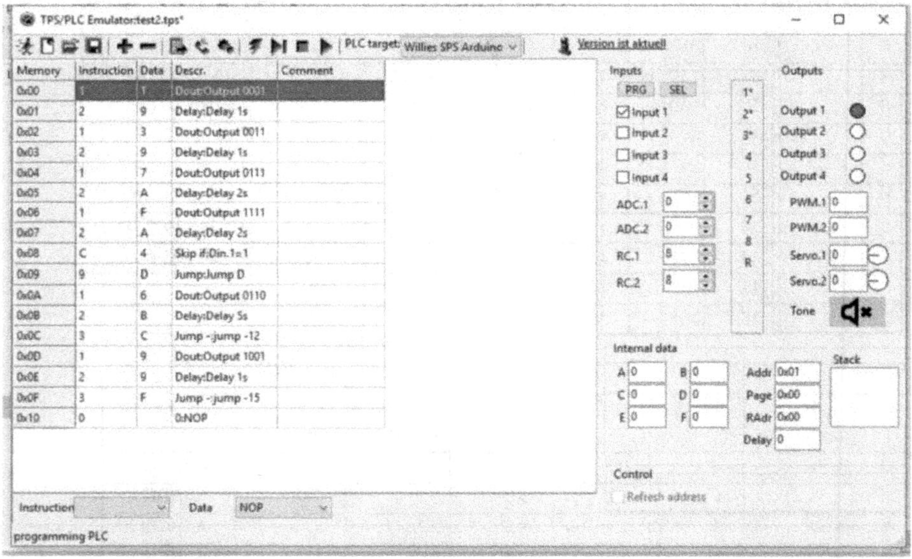

The emulator can work with the different instruction sets of different TPS versions.
On the left you can see the programming window.
This can either be typed in directly or generated via the two combo boxes below.
There you can select the possible commands – dependent on the target selected of the included versions.
The commands can then be executed via the 4 buttons in the top center block.
The first button tests the currently selected command (jumps are not carried out)
The second button executes the program in single-step mode.
The third button stops single-step mode
The fourth button is Start-Stop, to run at maximum speed.

In the left window you make the entries and view the results as you step through the program.

At the bottom you can see a few more the drop downs with the instructions.

.

On the right you can set inputs and see results at the outputs.

The lower block on the right shows what is happening internally in the simulated processor.

And additional documentation in English will be made available.

ATTENTION: The current version of Avira Antivirus has a false positive message.

9.5 - Arduino goes TPS **from Willie's website**

http://wkla.no-ip.biz/ArduinoWiki/doku.php?id=arduino:arduinosps

http://wk-music.de/ArduinoWiki/

You can switch between German and English

For my Lighthouse model (that I have sold in the meantime) I needed a circuit that flashes the light every 5 seconds 3x. Since the analog solution is not straightforward, I have dug out an ATTiny24 (I just had one available) from my hardware collection, switched on my AVR studio and just quickly wrote the controller software. A quick solution.

At various model exhibitions, I was asked again and again how to replicate it.

Of course you can, if you ...

And of course, other flash sequences should be selectable. And preferably controlled by remote control, selectable including other lamps ...

I am surprised that among the model DIYlers the MCU knowledge is rather scarce. That's a pity.

I recently came across Burkhard Kainka's TPS. This was just the right solution for many needs in model making. It is easy to program. Actually reduced to the bare minimum. The only thing the TPS lacks is the connection to a remote control. And also, the possibility to control one (or 2) servos the TPS does not have. Not yet, I thought to myself.

TPS original Kit still available, the Franzis Kit is not available anymore: https://www.conrad.com/ce/de/product/192286/Lernpaket-Conrad-Components-Profi-Mikrocontroller-10104-ab-14-Jahre

Original TPS Book English – new version planned including this information: https://www.amazon.co.uk/Learning-Programming-MyCo-easily-independent-ebook/dp/B00K6N87UG/ref=asap_bc?ie=UTF8

Where it all started: http://www.b-kainka.de/lpTPS.html

The original chip preprogrammed: http://www.ak-modul-bus.de/cgi-bin/iboshop.cgi?search,794654520073662

TPS Examples: http://www.elektronik-labor.de/Lernpakete/TPS/TPS0.html

And so I started:

Since I am very familiar with the Atmel processor range and also have a lot of experience with the Arduino system, it was only a small step to move the TPS functionality on to the Arduino.
In addition, the Arduino is very widespread.
At first, I thought I could easily adapt the existing TPS variant written in BASCOM, but unfortunately that was not so easy. So, I've reprogrammed the entire controller functionality from scatch and also added a few command extensions for the model design people. Here I present the resulting version free of charge and for general use. If you find a bug / mistake, then just write an email, so I can correct it. I have not been able to test all possible paths yet and will try to remove the bugs as soon as possible.

And something more regarding this Arduino implementation.
It can run on 2 different MCU's:
On the one hand, on the Arduino itself,
then even with the possibility to be programmed directly from my emulator.
(currently only on the Duemilanove)

The 2nd variant is based on an ATTiny84.
Unfortunately, this software can then only be programmed using a "standard" ISP programmer.
And the TPS commands are then programmed directly as with the HOLTEC version - only via the buttons and LEDs – no PC connection.
This possibility exists of course in the Arduino version as well, a good solution if you have to modify something quickly on-site close to the water with your model boats.

Connections:

SPS Connections	**Arduino Pins**
Dout1..4	**D4..D7**
Din1..4	*D0..D3*
ADC1,2	A1,2
PWM1,2	D9,10
RC1,2	D17,18 (A3,4)
Servo1,2	D9,10
SW_PRG	D8
SW_SEL	D11

A picture showing all of the Arduino external connections can be for example found at https://www.circuito.io/blog/arduino-uno-pinout/

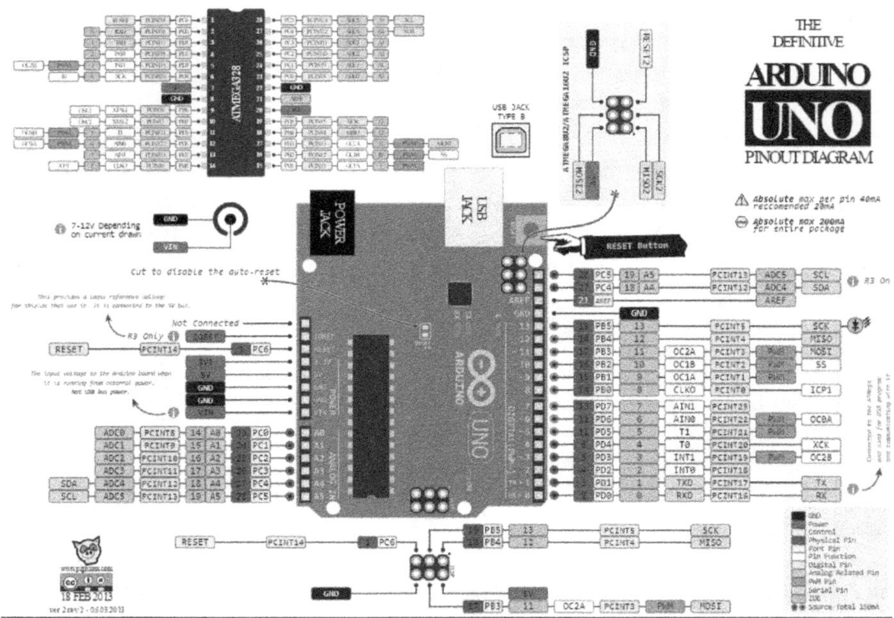

Features

In addition to Burkhard's TPS, this version has the following additional features:

☒ 2 RC channel outputs can be read and the PWM can be used as input for this TPS.

☒ 2 servo driving channels. There is the additional output for 2 RC servos. (Unfortunately, this automatically eliminates the usage of the two PWM Input channels.)

☒ Extensions of the instruction set. Now there are 1 byte instructions. This makes the reading and setting of ADC, RC, PWM, and servo much more sensitive with higher resolution.

☒ In addition, there is a new calculation. A = B * 16 + A to calculate 1 byte.

☒ There are also 2 additional registers for storing values;

☒ And a 16-level stack has been implemented with the two usual access methods: Push value onto stack and Pop from stack – read data and take the value off the stack.

☒ Regarding the Skip instruction, there is now as well the A = 0 condition

☒ And last but not least, you can define and start 6 different subroutines. These may then be located outside the 256-byte address space. For the Arduino, the EEPROM size is 1KB (ATMega328), while the ATTiny84 is 512 bytes in size.

The PWM signals are generated at 500Hz, the servo signals are PWM coded. (50Hz repetition frequency; and the shortest pulse is 1ms long, the longest pulse 2ms, middle position is at 1,5ms.)

The Arduino can be programmed via the keys as known from the TPS variant. But there is also the possibility to write programs via my TPS / SPS emulator and the software can be uploaded directly into the Arduino. Theoretically, this is also possible with the ATTiny variant, but for this solution there must be an ISP programmer available. With the Arduino solution everything is already on board.
Using the Arduino UNO, the whole thing should actually work immediately.
If somebody sponsors a Leonardo, I can adapt the PLC and the EMUlator for it as well.

Limitations

A mixed operation of servo and PWM (for example, PWM.1 and Servo.2) is unfortunately not possible because the two influence each other. So, either servo input or PWM output.

9.6 - Instruction Set

Areas shaded in yellow are extensions of my ArduinoSPS and ATTiny84 version.

	0	1	2	3	4	5	6	7
	n.n.	Port	Delay	Jump back relative	A=	„=A“	A=	A= Options
0	NOP	off	1ms	0	0	A<->B		
1		1	2ms	1	1	B=A	A=B	A=A + 1
2		2	5ms	2	2	C=A	A=C	A=A - 1
3		3	10ms	3	3	D=A	A=D	A=A + B
4		4	20ms	4	4	Dout=A	Din	A=A - B
5		5	50ms	5	5	Dout.0=A.0	Din.0	A=A * B
6		6	100ms	6	6	Dout.1=A.0	Din.1	A=A / B
7		7	200ms	7	7	Dout.2=A.0	Din.2	A=A and B
8		8	500ms	8	8	Dout.3=A.0	Din.3	A=A or B
9		9	1s	9	9	PWM.0=A	ADC.0	A=A xor B
a		10	2s	10	10	PWM.1=A	ADC.1	A= not A
b		11	5s	11	11	Servo.0=A	RCin.0	A= A % B (Rem.)
c		12	10s	12	12	Servo.1=A	RCin.1	A= A + 16 * B
d		13	20s	13	13	E=A	A=E	A= B - A
e		14	30s	14	14	F=A	A=F	
f		15	60s	15	15	Push A	Pop A	

Additional Features of the ArduinoSPS version:

☒ There are 2 additional registers (E and F)

☒ And there is a stack area with the 2 usual interface methods push (add to stack) and pop (take off the stack). There are 16 level positions in this stack.

☒ There are also 2 new calculations; one is the remainder of a division (A = A% B) and one an 8-bit conversion. A = A + 16 * B

☒ Since version 0.6, the swap command has also been added, swapping the A and B register contents.

☒ And a new calculation A = B - A. Especially, when you are working in an 8- bit space, it is sometimes quite cumbersome to carry out such an operation without.

8	9	a	b	c	d	e	f
Page	Jump absolute (#+ 16*page)	C* C>0: C=C-1; # + (16* page)	D*D> 0: D=D-1; # + (16* page)	Skip if	Call # + (16* Page)	Callsub /Ret	Byte Instr.
0	0	0	0	A=0	0	ret	A=ADC.0
1	1	1	1	A>B	1	Call 1	A=ADC.1
2	2	2	2	A<B	2	2	A=RCin.0
3	3	3	3	A=B	3	3	A=RCin.1
4	4	4	4	Din.0=1	4	4	PWM.0=A
5	5	5	5	Din.1=1	5	5	PWM.1=A
6	6	6	6	Din.2=1	6	6	Servo.0=A
7	7	7	7	Din.3=1	7		Servo.1=A
8	8	8	8	Din.0=0	8	Def 1	
9	9	9	9	Din.1=0	9	2	
10	10	10	10	Din.2=0	10	3	
11	11	11	11	Din.3=0	11	4	
12	12	12	12	S_PRG=0	12	5	
13	13	13	13	S_SEL=0	13	6	
14	14	14	14	S_PRG=1	14		
15	15	15	15	S_SEL=1	15	restart	PrgEnd

Aditional Features in this ArduinoSPS version:

☒ As we now have more EEPROM memory, the page area is been extended to 16 pages. So, you can now enter a program that is 256 bytes long.

☒ Regarding the Skip command, there is now as well the Skip command for condition A = 0.

☒ Via the E commands, you can now program 6 real subroutines. These are created using the Def# command. With Call# the routine is started. With Return you come back to the main program. The Def# may also be positioned above the 256 bytes in the EEPROM. So, also outside the range of the jump commands.

☒ Also new is the Restart command, which restarts the entire controller.

☒ In the F area, there are the new commands located, which work with the extended 8-bit resolution.

☒ FF means end of program. → and an automatic jump to program location 00.

And now please have fun with the ArduinoSPS.

Oh, and as always: everything without any warranty ...

And here the picture of a small test setup:

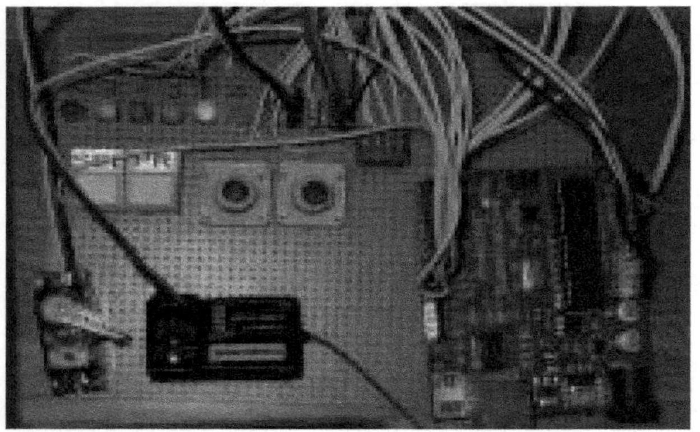

9.7 - Download

Arduino SPS Source

```
/*
 SPS System mit dem Arduino.

 Version 0.6
 - Stack auf 16 Bytes beschränkt;
   wird zu oft gepusht, werden die alten Werte rausgeschoben.

 Basiert auf dem TPS System vom elektronik-labor.

 Erweiterungen:
 - es können bis zu 6 Unterroutinen definiert werden
   und diese direkt angesprungen werden.

 - neben Return gibt's jetzt auch einen Restart

 - 2 Servo Ausgänge für übliche RC Servos. (10°
    Auflösung in Nibble Modus,
    1° Auflösung im Bytemodus)

   ACHTUNG: Servo Inputs und PWM Ausgänge
   sind nicht mischbar
   und können auch nicht gleichzeitig benutzt werden.

 - 2 RC Eingänge
   ( 16  Schritte Auflösung im nibble Modus, Mitte 8,
    255 Schritte im Byte Modus)

 - funktioniert auch mit einem ATTiny84
   (44 ist leider auf Grund der Programmgröße
   nicht mehr für den erweiterten Befehlssatz möglich)

 - Call stack von bis zu 16 Unterfunktionen

 - Neue Register E und F
*/
```

```
/*
PLC system using the Arduino.

Version 0.6
 - Stack depth is limited to 16 bytes, if too many values are pushed,
   the old values are pushed out of the 16 byte range.

 - Based on the TPS system of Burkhard Kainka's  electronics lab.

Extensions:

 - Up to 6 subroutines can be defined and these directly be jumped to.

 - Bin addition to Return, there's also a Restart command

 - 2 servo outputs for common RC servos.
   (10° resolution in nibble mode,
    1° resolution in byte mode)

   ATTENTION: Servo and PWM outputs cannot be mixed
   and can also not used at the same time.

 - 2 RC inputs
   (16 steps resolution in nibble mode,middle status 8,
   255 steps in byte mode)

 - Also works with an ATTiny84
  (44 is unfortunately not possible as of program size
   for the extended instruction set)

 - Call stack of up to 16 subroutines

 - new additional registers E and F
 */
```

```
#include <EEPROM.h>
#include <avr/eeprom.h>
#include <Servo.h>

// Program im Debugmodus kompilieren, dann werden zusaetzliche
// Ausgaben
//  auf die serielle Schnittstelle geschrieben.

// Compile programs in Debug Mode, then additional output data
// will be
// written to the serial port.

//#define debug

#ifdef debug
#define dbgOut(S) \
Serial.print(S);
#define dbgOutLn(S) \
Serial.println(S);
#else
#define dbgOut(S)
#define dbgOutLn(S)
#endif

// Hier wird definiert, ob die zusaetzlichen Erweiterungen
// der Willie SPS aktiv sind oder nicht.

// Here is defined whether the additional extensions
// of the Willie PLC are active or not.

#define SPS_ENHANCEMENT

// Befehle
// Instructions

const byte PORT = 0x10;
const byte DELAY = 0x20;
const byte JUMP_BACK = 0x30;
```

```
const byte SET_A = 0x40;
const byte IS_A = 0x50;
const byte A_IS = 0x60;
const byte CALC = 0x70;
const byte PAGE = 0x80;
const byte JUMP = 0x90;
const byte C_COUNT = 0xA0;
const byte D_COUNT = 0xB0;
const byte SKIP_IF = 0xC0;
const byte CALL = 0xD0;
const byte CALL_SUB = 0xE0;
const byte CMD_BYTE = 0xF0;

// Hardwareanbindung
// Hardware connections

#ifndef __AVR_ATtinyX4__

// Arduino Hardware

const byte Dout_0 = 4;
const byte Dout_1 = 5;
const byte Dout_2 = 6;
const byte Dout_3 = 7;

const byte Din_0 = 0;
const byte Din_1 = 1;
const byte Din_2 = 2;
const byte Din_3 = 3;
const byte ADC_0 = 1;
const byte ADC_1 = 2;
const byte PWM_1 = 9;
const byte PWM_2 = 10;
const byte RC_0 = 17;
const byte RC_1 = 18;
const byte SERVO_1 = 9;
const byte SERVO_2 = 10;
```

```
const byte SW_PRG = 8;
const byte SW_SEL = 11;
const byte ADC_KEY = 0;

#else
// ATTiny84 Hardware
const byte Dout_0 = 6;
const byte Dout_1 = 5;
const byte Dout_2 = 4;
const byte Dout_3 = 1;
const byte Din_0 = 10;
const byte Din_1 = 9;
const byte Din_2 = 8;
const byte Din_3 = 7;
const byte ADC_0 = 0;
const byte ADC_1 = 1;
const byte PWM_1 = 2;
const byte PWM_2 = 3;
const byte RC_0 = 10;
const byte RC_1 = 9;
const byte SERVO_1 = 2;
const byte SERVO_2 = 3;

const byte SW_PRG = 0;
const byte SW_SEL = 8;
const byte ADC_KEY = 0;
#endif

const int  adc_key_val[5] ={
  30, 150, 360, 535, 760 };
const int NUM_KEYS = 5;
const byte KEY_RIGHT = 0;
const byte KEY_UP = 1;
const byte KEY_DOWN = 2;
const byte KEY_LEFT = 3;
const byte KEY_SELECT = 4;

// debouncing with 100ms
const byte DEBOUNCE = 100;
```

```
const byte subCnt = 7;
word subs[subCnt];

int adc_key_in;
int key=-1;
int oldkey=-1;

word addr;
word page;

#ifdef SPS_ENHANCEMENT
const byte SAVE_CNT = 16;
#else
const byte SAVE_CNT = 1;
#endif

word saveaddr[SAVE_CNT];
byte saveCnt;

#ifdef SPS_ENHANCEMENT
byte stack[SAVE_CNT];
byte stackCnt;
#endif

unsigned long tmpValue;

boolean prgMode;
byte a,b,c,d;

#ifdef SPS_ENHANCEMENT
byte e,f;
#endif

#ifdef SPS_ENHANCEMENT
Servo servo1;
Servo servo2;
#endif
```

```
byte prog = 0;
byte data = 0;
byte com = 0;

void setup() {
  pinMode(Dout_0, OUTPUT);
  pinMode(Dout_1, OUTPUT);
  pinMode(Dout_2, OUTPUT);
  pinMode(Dout_3, OUTPUT);

  pinMode(PWM_1, OUTPUT);
  pinMode(PWM_2, OUTPUT);

  pinMode(Din_0, INPUT);
  digitalWrite(Din_0, HIGH);
  pinMode(Din_1, INPUT);
  digitalWrite(Din_1, HIGH);
  pinMode(Din_2, INPUT);
  digitalWrite(Din_2, HIGH);
  pinMode(Din_3, INPUT);
  digitalWrite(Din_3, HIGH);

  pinMode(SW_PRG, INPUT);
  digitalWrite(SW_PRG, HIGH);
  pinMode(SW_SEL, INPUT);
  digitalWrite(SW_SEL, HIGH);

  // Serielle Schnittstelle einstellen
  // Setup Serial Interface


#ifndef __AVR_ATtinyX4__
#ifdef debug
  Serial.begin(19200);
  Serial.flush();
  delay(100);
#endif
#endif
```

```
  //  writeProgram();
  doReset();

  prgMode = digitalRead(SW_PRG) == 0;
}

void doReset() {
  dbgOutLn("Reset");
#ifdef SPS_ENHANCEMENT
  servo1.detach();
  servo2.detach();
#endif

  for (int i = 0; i < subCnt; i++) {
    subs[i] = 0;
  }

  readProgram();

  addr = 0;
  page = 0;
  saveCnt = 0;
  a = 0;
  b = 0;
  c = 0;
  d = 0;
#ifdef SPS_ENHANCEMENT
  e = 0;
  f = 0;
#endif
}

/*
getting all addresses of sub programms
 */
void readProgram() {
  dbgOutLn("Read program");
  word addr = 0;
  for ( addr = 0; addr <= E2END; addr++) {
```

```
    byte value = EEPROM.read(addr);
#ifdef debug
    Serial.print(value, HEX);
    if (((addr+1) % 16) == 0) {
      dbgOutLn();
    }
    else {
      dbgOut(",");
    }
#endif
    if (value == 0xFF) {
      // ende des Programms
      break;
    }
    byte cmd = (value & 0xF0);
    byte data = (value & 0x0F);
#ifdef debug
    Serial.print("(");
    Serial.print(cmd, HEX);
    Serial.print(data, HEX);
    Serial.print(")");
#endif

    if (cmd == CALL_SUB) {
      if (data >=8) {
        data = data - 8;
        subs[data] = addr + 1;
      }
    }
#ifdef SPS_ENHANCEMENT
    if ((cmd == IS_A) && (data == 0x0B)) {
      dbgOutLn("attach Srv1");
      servo1.attach(SERVO_1);
    }
    if ((cmd == CMD_BYTE) && (data == 0x06)) {
      dbgOutLn("attach Srv1");
      servo1.attach(SERVO_1);
    }
    if ((cmd == IS_A) && (data == 0x0C)) {
```

```
        dbgOutLn("attach Srv2");
        servo2.attach(SERVO_2);
      }
      if ((cmd == CMD_BYTE) && (data == 0x07)) {
        dbgOutLn("attach Srv2");
        servo2.attach(SERVO_2);
      }
#endif
  }
  dbgOutLn();
}

/*
main loop
 */
void loop() {
  dbgOutLn("l");
  if (prgMode) {
    programMode();
  }
  else {
    byte value = EEPROM.read(addr);
    byte cmd = (value & 0xF0);
    byte data = (value & 0x0F);
#ifdef debug
    Serial.print(addr, HEX);
    Serial.print(":");
    Serial.print(value,HEX);
    Serial.print(",");
    Serial.print(cmd,HEX);
    Serial.print(",");
    Serial.println(data,HEX);
#endif
    addr = addr + 1;
    switch (cmd) {
    case PORT:
      doPort(data);
      break;
    case DELAY:
```

```
    doDelay(data);
    break;
  case JUMP_BACK:
    doJumpBack(data);
    break;
  case SET_A:
    doSetA(data);
    break;
  case A_IS:
    doAIs(data);
    break;
  case IS_A:
    doIsA(data);
    break;
  case CALC:
    doCalc(data);
    break;
  case PAGE:
    doPage(data);
    break;
  case JUMP:
    doJump(data);
    break;
  case C_COUNT:
    doCCount(data);
    break;
  case D_COUNT:
    doDCount(data);
    break;
  case SKIP_IF:
    doSkipIf(data);
    break;
  case CALL:
    doCall(data);
    break;
  case CALL_SUB:
    doCallSub(data);
    break;
  case CMD_BYTE:
```

```
      doByte(data);
      break;
    default:
      ;
    }
    if (addr > E2END) {
      doReset();
    }
  }
  //  delay(500);
}

/*
output to port
 */
void doPort(byte data) {
  digitalWrite(Dout_0,(data & 0x01)>0);
  digitalWrite(Dout_1,(data & 0x02)>0);
  digitalWrite(Dout_2,(data & 0x04)>0);
  digitalWrite(Dout_3,(data & 0x08)>0);
}

/*
delay in ms
 */
void doDelay(byte data) {
  switch (data) {
  case 0:
    delay(1);
    break;
  case 1:
    delay(2);
    break;
  case 2:
    delay(5);
    break;
  case 3:
    delay(10);
    break;
```

```
case 4:
  delay(20);
  break;
case 5:
  delay(50);
  break;
case 6:
  delay(100);
  break;
case 7:
  delay(200);
  break;
case 8:
  delay(500);
  break;
case 9:
  delay(1000);
  break;
case 10:
  delay(2000);
  break;
case 11:
  delay(5000);
  break;
case 12:
  delay(10000);
  break;
case 13:
  delay(20000);
  break;
case 14:
  delay(30000);
  break;
case 15:
  delay(60000);
  break;
default:
  break;
}
```

```
}

/*
jump back relative
 */
void doJumpBack(byte data) {
  addr = addr - data - 1;
}

/*
a = data
 */
void doSetA(byte data) {
  a = data;
}

/*
a = somthing;
 */
void doAIs(byte data) {
  switch (data) {
  case 1:
    a = b;
    break;
  case 2:
    a = c;
    break;
  case 3:
    a = d;
    break;
  case 4:
    a = Din_0 + (Din_1 << 1) + (Din_2 << 2) + (Din_3 << 3);
    break;
  case 5:
    a = Din_0;
    break;
  case 6:
    a = Din_1;
    break;
```

```
  case 7:
    a = Din_2;
    break;
  case 8:
    a = Din_3;
    break;
  case 9:
    tmpValue = analogRead(ADC_0);
    a = tmpValue / 64;
//(Umrechnen auf 4 bit)( recalculate to 4 bit )
    break;
  case 10:
    tmpValue = analogRead(ADC_1);
    a = tmpValue / 64;
//(Umrechnen auf 4 bit) ( recalculate to 4 bit )
    break;
#ifdef SPS_ENHANCEMENT
  case 11:
    tmpValue = pulseIn(RC_0,HIGH, 100000);
    if (tmpValue < 1000) {
      tmpValue = 1000;
    }
    if (tmpValue > 2000) {
      tmpValue = 2000;
    }
    a = (tmpValue - 1000) / 64;
//(Umrechnen auf 4 bit)( recalculate to 4 bit )
    dbgOut("RC1:");
    dbgOut(tmpValue);
    dbgOut("=");
    dbgOutLn(a);
    break;
  case 12:
    tmpValue = pulseIn(RC_1,HIGH, 100000);
    if (tmpValue < 1000) {
      tmpValue = 1000;
    }
    if (tmpValue > 2000) {
      tmpValue = 2000;
```

```
    }
    a = (tmpValue - 1000) / 64;
    //(Umrechnen auf 4 bit)( recalculate to 4 bit )

    dbgOut("RC2:");
    dbgOut(tmpValue);
    dbgOut("=");
    dbgOutLn(a);
    break;
  case 13:
    a = e;
    break;
  case 14:
    a = f;
    break;
  case 15:
    if (stackCnt > 0) {
      stackCnt -= 1;
      a = stack[stackCnt];
    }
    else {
      a = 0;
    }
    break;
#endif
  default:
    break;
  }
}

/*
somthing = a;
 */
void doIsA(byte data) {
  switch (data) {
  case 1:
    b = a;
    break;
  case 2:
```

```
      c = a;
      break;
    case 3:
      d = a;
      break;
    case 4:
      doPort(a);
      break;
    case 5:
      digitalWrite(Dout_0,(a && 0x01) > 0);
      break;
    case 6:
      digitalWrite(Dout_1,(a && 0x01) > 0);
      break;
    case 7:
      digitalWrite(Dout_2,(a && 0x01) > 0);
      break;
    case 8:
      digitalWrite(Dout_3,(a && 0x01) > 0);
      break;
    case 9:
      tmpValue = a * 16;
      dbgOut("PWM1:");
      dbgOutLn(tmpValue);
      analogWrite(PWM_1, tmpValue);
      break;
    case 10:
      tmpValue = a * 16;
      dbgOut("PWM2:");
      dbgOutLn(tmpValue);
      analogWrite(PWM_2, tmpValue);
      break;
#ifdef SPS_ENHANCEMENT
    case 11:
      if (servo1.attached()) {
        dbgOut("Srv1:");
        dbgOutLn((a*10) + 10);
        servo1.write((a*10) + 10);
      }
```

```
    break;
  case 12:
    if (servo2.attached()) {
      dbgOut("Srv2:");
      dbgOutLn((a*10) + 10);
      servo2.write((a*10) + 10);
    }
    break;
  case 13:
    e = a;
    break;
  case 14:
    f = a;
    break;
  case 15:
    if (stackCnt < SAVE_CNT) {
      stack[stackCnt] = a;
      stackCnt += 1;
    }
    else {
      for (int i = 1; i <= SAVE_CNT; i++) {
        stack[i-1] = stack[i];
      }
      stack[stackCnt] = a;
    }
    break;
#endif
  default:
    break;
  }
}

/*
calculations
 */
void doCalc(byte data) {
  switch (data) {
  case 1:
    a = a + 1;
```

```
    break;
  case 2:
    a = a - 1;
    break;
  case 3:
    a = a + b;
    break;
  case 4:
    a = a - b;
    break;
  case 5:
    a = a * b;
    break;
  case 6:
    a = a / b;
    break;
  case 7:
    a = a & b;
    break;
  case 8:
    a = a | b;
    break;
  case 9:
    a = a ^ b;
    break;
  case 10:
    a = !a;
    break;
#ifdef SPS_ENHANCEMENT
  case 11:
    a = a % b;
    break;
  case 12:
    a = a + 16 * b;
    break;
#endif
  default:
    break;
  }
```

```
}

/*
setting page
 */
void doPage(byte data) {
  page = data * 16;
}

/*
jump absolute
 */
void doJump(byte data) {
  addr = page + data;
}

/*
counting with c register
 */
void doCCount(byte data) {
  if (c > 0) {
    c -= 1;
    c = c && 0x0F;
    doJump(data);
  }
}

/*
counting with d register
 */
void doDCount(byte data) {
  if (d > 0) {
    d -= 1;
    d = d && 0x0F;
    doJump(data);
  }
}

/*
```

```
 simple comdition = true skip next command
 */
void doSkipIf(byte data) {
  switch (data) {
#ifdef SPS_ENHANCEMENT
  case 0:
    if (a == 0) {
      addr += 1;
    };
    break;
#endif
  case 1:
    if (a > b) {
      addr += 1;
    };
    break;
  case 2:
    if (a < b) {
      addr += 1;
    };
    break;
  case 3:
    if (a == b) {
      addr += 1;
    };
    break;
  case 4:
    tmpValue = digitalRead(Din_0);
    if (tmpValue == 1) {
      addr += 1;
    };
    break;
  case 5:
    tmpValue = digitalRead(Din_1);
    if (tmpValue == 1) {
      addr += 1;
    };
    break;
  case 6:
```

```
    tmpValue = digitalRead(Din_2);
    if (tmpValue == 1) {
      addr += 1;
    };
    break;
  case 7:
    tmpValue = digitalRead(Din_3);
    if (tmpValue == 1) {
      addr += 1;
    };
    break;
  case 8:
    tmpValue = digitalRead(Din_0);
    if (tmpValue == 0) {
      addr += 1;
    };
    break;
  case 9:
    tmpValue = digitalRead(Din_1);
    if (tmpValue == 0) {
      addr += 1;
    };
    break;
  case 10:
    tmpValue = digitalRead(Din_2);
    if (tmpValue == 0) {
      addr += 1;
    };
    break;
  case 11:
    tmpValue = digitalRead(Din_3);
    if (tmpValue == 0) {
      addr += 1;
    };
    break;
  case 12:
    tmpValue = digitalRead(SW_PRG);
    if (tmpValue == 0) {
      addr += 1;
```

```
      };
      break;
    case 13:
      tmpValue = digitalRead(SW_SEL);
      if (tmpValue == 0) {
        addr += 1;
      };
      break;
    case 14:
      tmpValue = digitalRead(SW_PRG);
      if (tmpValue == 1) {
        addr += 1;
      };
      break;
    case 15:
      tmpValue = digitalRead(SW_SEL);
      if (tmpValue == 1) {
        addr += 1;
      };
      break;
    default:
      break;
  }
}

/*
calling a subroutine
 */
void doCall(byte data) {
  saveaddr[saveCnt] = addr;
  saveCnt += 1;
  addr = page + data;
}

/*
calling a subroutine, calling return and restart
 */
void doCallSub(byte data) {
  if (data == 0) {
```

```
    if (saveCnt < 0) {
      doReset();
      return;
    }
    saveCnt -= 1;
    addr = saveaddr[saveCnt];
    return;
  }
#ifdef SPS_ENHANCEMENT
  if (data <= 7) {
    // call subroutine number
    saveaddr[saveCnt] = addr;
    saveCnt += 1;
    addr = subs[data-1];
    return;
  }
  if (data == 0x0f) {
    doReset();
  }
#endif
}

/*
calling a subroutine, calling return and restart
 */
void doByte(byte data) {
#ifdef SPS_ENHANCEMENT
  dbgOut("B ");
  switch (data) {
  case 0:
    tmpValue = analogRead(ADC_0);
    a = tmpValue / 4;
      // (Umrechnen auf 4 bit) ( recalculate to 4 bit )

    break;
  case 1:
    tmpValue = analogRead(ADC_1);
    a = tmpValue / 4;
      // (Umrechnen auf 4 bit) ( recalculate to 4 bit )
```

```
    break;
  case 2:
    tmpValue = pulseIn(RC_0,HIGH, 100000);
    if (tmpValue < 1000) {
      tmpValue = 1000;
    }
    if (tmpValue > 2000) {
      tmpValue = 2000;
    }
    a = (tmpValue - 1000) / 4;
      //(Umrechnen auf 4 bit)( recalculate to 4 bit )

    dbgOut("RC1:");
    dbgOut(tmpValue);
    dbgOut("=");
    dbgOutLn(a);
    break;
  case 3:
    tmpValue = pulseIn(RC_1,HIGH, 100000);
    if (tmpValue < 1000) {
      tmpValue = 1000;
    }
    if (tmpValue > 2000) {
      tmpValue = 2000;
    }
    a = (tmpValue - 1000) / 4;
      //(Umrechnen auf 4 bit)( recalculate to 4 bit )

    dbgOut("RC2:");
    dbgOut(tmpValue);
    dbgOut("=");
    dbgOutLn(a);
    break;
  case 4:
    tmpValue = a;
    dbgOut("PWM1:");
    dbgOutLn(a);
    analogWrite(PWM_1, a);
```

```
      break;
    case 5:
      tmpValue = a;
      dbgOut("PWM2:");
      dbgOutLn(a);
      analogWrite(PWM_2, a);
      break;
    case 6:
      if (servo1.attached()) {
        dbgOut("Srv1:");
        dbgOutLn(a);
        tmpValue = (180 * a) / 255;
        servo1.write(tmpValue);
      }
      break;
    case 7:
      if (servo2.attached()) {
        dbgOut("Srv2:");
        dbgOutLn(a);
        tmpValue = (180 * a) / 255;
        servo2.write(tmpValue);
      }
      break;
  }
#endif
}

// Convert ADC value to key number
int getKey(byte input)
{
  int k;
  for (k = 0; k < NUM_KEYS; k++)
  {
    if (input < adc_key_val[k])
    {
      return k;
    }
  }
  if (k >= NUM_KEYS)
```

```
    k = -1;                 // No valid key pressed
  return k;
}

void lighting() {
  doPort(0x0F);
  delay(200);
}
/*
entering the programming mode
 */
void programMode() {
  // checking if advance programmer board connected?
#ifdef SPS_ENHANCEMENT
  key = getKey(ADC_KEY);
  if (key != oldkey)       // if keypress is detected
  {
    delay(50);            // wait for debounce time
    if (key == KEY_SELECT) {
      advanceProgramming();
    }
  }
#endif
  dbgOutLn("PrgMode");
  addr = 0;
  do {
    dbgOut("Adr:");
    dbgOutLn(addr);
    // LoNibble Adresse anzeigen
    doPort(addr);
    delay(300);
    lighting();
    // HiNibble Adresse anzeigen
    data = (addr & 0xf0) >> 4;
      //Adresse anzeigen   // Display Address
    doPort(data);
    delay(300);
    lighting();
```

```
byte Eebyte = EEPROM.read(addr);
data = Eebyte & 15;
com = Eebyte >> 4;
doPort(com); //Befehl anzeigen
digitalWrite(PWM_1,HIGH);
do {
}
while (digitalRead(SW_SEL) == 1); // S2 = 1
delay(DEBOUNCE);

prog = 1;
  //Phase 1: Befehl anzeigen
  //Phase 1: Display Instruction
do {
  dbgOut("C:");
  dbgOut(com);
  dbgOut(", D:");
  dbgOut(data);
  dbgOut(", P:");
  dbgOutLn(prog);

  if (digitalRead(SW_PRG) == 0) {
    if (prog == 1) {
      prog = 2;
      com = 15;
    }
    if (prog == 2) {
  //Phase 2: Befehl verändert
  //Phase2: Instruct. changed
      com = com + 1;
      com = com & 15;
      doPort(com);
      digitalWrite(PWM_1,HIGH);
    }
    if (prog == 3) {
  //Phase 3: Befehl unverändert, Daten ändern
  // Phase3: Instruction unchanged, change Data
      prog = 5;
      data = 15;
```

```
  }
  if (prog == 4) {
//Phase 4: Befehl und Daten geändert
// Phase4: Instruction and Data changed
    prog = 5;
    data = 15;
  }
  if (prog == 5) {
//Phase 5: Daten verändert
// Phase5: Data changed
    data += 1;
    data = data & 15;
    doPort(data);
    digitalWrite(PWM_1,LOW);
  }
  delay(DEBOUNCE);
  do {
  }
  while(digitalRead(SW_PRG) == 1);
  delay(DEBOUNCE);
}

if (digitalRead(SW_SEL) == 0) {
  if (prog == 3) {
    prog = 7;
// nur angezeigt, nicht verändert
// only displayed, not changed
  }
  if (prog == 4) {
    doPort(255 - data);
    digitalWrite(PWM_1,LOW);
    prog = 6;
  }
  if (prog == 2) {
    doPort(data);
// Portd = Dat Or &HF0
    digitalWrite(PWM_1,LOW);
    prog = 4;
  }
```

```
      if (prog == 6) {
    // nur Kommando wurde verändert

    // only Instruction has changed
        data = data & 15;
        Eebyte = com * 16;
        Eebyte = Eebyte + data;
        EEPROM.write(addr,Eebyte);// Writeeeprom Eebyte, Addr
        doPort(0x0F);
        delay(600);
        addr += 1;
        prog = 0;
      }
      if (prog == 5) {
    //Daten wurden verändert
    // data has changed
        data = data & 15;
        Eebyte = com * 16;
        Eebyte = Eebyte + data;
        EEPROM.write(addr,Eebyte);
    //           Writeeeprom Eebyte , Addr
        doPort(0xF0);
        delay(600);
        addr += 1;
        prog = 0;
      }
      if (prog == 7) {
        addr += 1;
        prog = 0;
      }
      delay(DEBOUNCE);
      do {
      }
      while (digitalRead(SW_SEL) == 0);
      delay(DEBOUNCE);
    }
  }
  while (prog != 0);
}
```

```
  while(true);
}

void advanceProgramming() {
}

void showHex() {

}
         //   End of Software
```

9.8 - TPS/MyCo-A 4-Bit SPS to learn Programming

in SW or using HOLTEK http://wk-music.de/ArduinoWiki/ Part 1

	0	1	2	3	4	5	6	7
	n.n.	Port	Delay	Ju <- rel	A=	„=A“	A=	A=Calculations
0	NOP	0	1ms	0	0	A<->B		
1		1	2ms	1	1	B=A	A=B	A=A + 1
2		2	5ms	2	2	C=A	A=C	A=A - 1
3		3	10ms	3	3	D=A	A=D	A=A + B
4		4	20ms	4	4	Dout=A	Din	A=A - B
5		5	50ms	5	5	Dout.0=A.0	Din.0	A=A * B
6		6	100ms	6	6	Dout.1=A.0	Din.1	A=A / B
7		7	200ms	7	7	Dout.2=A.0	Din.2	A=A AND B
8		8	500ms	8	8	Dout.3=A.0	Din.3	A=A OR B
9		9	1s	9	9	PWM.0=A	ADC.0	A=A XOR B
A		10	2s	10	10		ADC.1	A= NOT A
B		11	5s	11	11			
C		12	10s	12	12			
D		13	20s	13	13			
E		14	30s	14	14			
F		15	60s	15	15			

And Part 2

8	9	A	B	C	D	E	F
Page	JMP	C*	D*	Skip if	Ca	RET	.
0	0	0	0		0	0	
1	1	1	1	A>B	1	1	
2	2	2	2	A<B	2	2	
3	3	3	3	A=B	3	3	
4	4	4	4	Din.0=1	4	4	
5	5	5	5	Din.1=1	5	5	
6	6	6	6	Din.2=1	6	6	
7	7	7	7	Din.3=1	7	7	
	8	8	8	Din.0=0	8	8	
	9	9	9	Din.1=0	9	9	
	10	10	10	Din.2=0	10	A	
	11	11	11	Din.3=0	11	B	
	12	12	12	S_PRG=0	12	C	
	13	13	13	S_SEL=0	13	D	
	14	14	14	S_PRG=1	14	E	
	15	15	15	S_SEL=1	15	F	FF

SPS
3 2 1 0
INPUT
Reg A
Reg B
ALU
Reg C
Reg D
OUT
PagReg
ProCtr
Delay
Skip
3 2 1 0

TPS / MyCo - A 4-Bit SPS to learn Programming – in SW only

or running on Arduino http://wk-music.de/ArduinoWiki/

	0	1	2	3	4	5	6	7
	n.n.	Port	Delay	Ju <- rel	A=	„=A"	A=	A=Calculations
0	NOP	0	1ms	0	0	A<->B		
1		1	2ms	1	1	B=A	A=B	A=A + 1
2		2	5ms	2	2	C=A	A=C	A=A - 1
3		3	10ms	3	3	D=A	A=D	A=A + B
4		4	20ms	4	4	Dout=A	Din	A=A - B
5		5	50ms	5	5	Dout.0=A.0	Din.0	A=A * B
6		6	100ms	6	6	Dout.1=A.0	Din.1	A=A / B
7		7	200ms	7	7	Dout.2=A.0	Din.2	A=A AND B
8		8	500ms	8	8	Dout.3=A.0	Din.3	A=A OR B
9		9	1s	9	9	PWM.0=A	ADC.0	A=A XOR B
A		10	2s	10	10	PWM.1=A	ADC.1	A= NOT A
B		11	5s	11	11	Servo.0=A	RCin.0	A= A % B (Rest)
C		12	10s	12	12	Servo.1=A	RCin.1	A= A + 16 * B
D		13	20s	13	13	E=A	A=E	A= B - A
E		14	30s	14	14	F=A	A=F	
F		15	60s	15	15	Push A	Pop A	

X9 Jump absolut (#+16*page), X10 C* C>0: C=C-1; # + (16*page)

X11 D*D>0:D=D-1; # + (16*page) XD Call # + (16*Page)

8	9	A	B	C	D	E	F
Page	X9	X10	X11	Skip if		Call /Ret	Byte Instr.
0	0	0	0	A=0	0	Ret	A=ADC.0
1	1	1	1	A>B	1	Call1	A=ADC.1
2	2	2	2	A<B	2	Call2	A=RCin.0
3	3	3	3	A=B	3	Call3	A=RCin.1
4	4	4	4	Din.0=1	4	Call4	PWM.0=A
5	5	5	5	Din.1=1	5	Call5	PWM.1=A
6	6	6	6	Din.2=1	6	Call6	Servo.0=A
7	7	7	7	Din.3=1	7		Servo.1=A
8	8	8	8	Din.0=0	8	Def1	
9	9	9	9	Din.1=0	9	Def2	
10	10	10	10	Din.2=0	10	Def3	
11	11	11	11	Din.3=0	11	Def4	
12	12	12	12	S_PRG=0	12	Def5	
13	13	13	13	S_SEL=0	13	Def6	
14	14	14	14	S_PRG=1	14		
15	15	15	15	S_SEL=1	15	Restart	PrgEnd

SPS
3 2 1 0
INPUT
Reg A
Reg B
ALU
Reg C
Reg D
Reg E
Reg F
OUT
PageReg
Prog.Ctr
Delay
Skip
3 2 1 0

10 - TPS / MyCo written in Forth

As you might have seen in one of the first pages, most of the books I publish are related to the language FORTH.
When the first version was written, I just got into Forth again after a long time.
I got great help from Michael Kalus, who could be convinced to emulate Burkhard Kainka's TPS in Forth, written for the TI MSP430 in a 20-pin package.
This then led to the MicroBox, a small board plus the option of a header board – which as you can see now, exactly has the 3 switches and 4LEDs plus one for PWM output.
All of the TPS functions can be replicated, but here you actually have a complete FORTH Interpreter/Compiler ON the chip as well. There is a command to exit the "local" function control of the 3 switches to the serial terminal function.
The extension of this book adds the opportunity to include the Forth code now, so people can give it a go and understand Forth code.
A good starting point would be to look at the documetation at

http://wiki.forth-ev.de/doku.php/en:projects:a-start-with-forth:start

For the eBook / Print Book, see the Forth Bookshelf at
https://www.amazon.co.uk/Juergen-Pintaske/e/B00N8HVEZM

Here the code that had been running on these boards.

To Flash the initial program into the chip needs the TI Launchpad connected to the PC. Afterwards the chip is independent just needing a USBtoSERIAL – or if just used as controller with the TPS Interface and nothing else is needed.
See pictures on page 118.

```
\ MyCo \ using 4e4th Release0.34b
\ Version 0.91 - edit pages using only S2 and S1.
\ started: 2014_08_10 now 2015_03_28

\ Achtung:
\ Zweistellige Ziffern sind Kommandos in MYCO !!
\ Willst du Zahlen eingeben, müssen Nullen davor sein.
\ Beispiel:
\ 59 lädt Register A in das PWM-Register.
```

```
\ 0059 legt den Zahlenwert 59 auf den Datenstack.

\ Careful:
\ Two-digit numbers are commands in MYCO !!
\ If you want to enter numbers, zeros must be in front of them.
\ Example:
\ 59 loads register A into the PWM register.
\ 0059 places the number 59 on the data stack.


\ Issues:
\ WIPE strikes after EDIT ;         fixed 24.02.2015
\ ugly EDIT; made a better one;     12.10.2014
\ S1 and S2 input faild sometimes; fixed 12.10.2014
\ STEP does wrong dumping;          fixed 08.10.2014


\ ++++++++++++++++++++++++++++++++++++++++++++++++++++++++++++
\
\ Start of the Program  MyCo, programmed in Forth
\ Based on Burkard Kainka's TPS, Juergen Pintaske
\ translated the German Manual into English and extended it.

\ This program in Forth simulates a very small processor, running
\ in a Franzis Kit which is planned to help Learning Programming;
\ and we use it here as an example of how to program the TI
\ MSP430 Controller. Owners of this Franzis kit can just add a
\ programmed MSP430G2553 and a reset resistor and replace the Holtek.
\ And all three options can be used to learn:
\   First, use the original TPS, running on a Holtek Processor,
\      and with the Hardware available from Franzis or Conrad.
\   Second, use the existing Hardware, take the Holtek chip out
\      and add a little board with the MSP430 Controller on it.
\      Just jumper the necessary wires to the preprogrammed MSP430.
\   Third, get a programmed MSP430 controller, add the 5 resistor LED
\      combinations and the 3 switches to 430 board,
\      and run completely in the MSP430,
\      but in addition
\      now with aserial
\      terminal control, showing on screen what actually happens
\      internally in all of the simulated processor registers.
\ This all looks like an overkill, but the target is here:
\ Learn Programming in a language called Forth
\ -  so as an Application.
```

```
\ A Note when using the serial terminal function:
\ Use the hex numbers only with preceding zeros.
\ Any hex XX without a proceeding 0 is interpreted as a command.
\ Example:
\ 71 is the command A<=A+1, 0071 is interpreted as a number.

\ Defining the I/O for this application

\ Device Pinout: MSP430G2553 20-Pin PDIP
\                       (TOP VIEW)

\ VCC----+3.3V--------[01   20]--Ground-----------VSS
\ (LED1 LP) AD1 P1.0--[02   19]--P2.6 OUT2 - 470R  + LED to GND
\ RXD-----------P1.1--[03   18]--P2.7 OUT3 - 470R  + LED to GND
\ TXD-----------P1.2--[04   17]--test
\ S2 to GND     P1.3--[05   16]--RST      S1-LP          to GND
\ ..........AD2 P1.4--[06   15]--P1.7     S1             to GND
\ _-_-_-_-_-FRQ P1.5--[07   14]--P1.6 PWM  - 470R  + LED to GND
\ ----------IN0 P2.0--[08   13]--P2.5 OUT1 - 470R  + LED to GND
\ ----------IN1 P2.1--[09   12]--P2.4 OUT0 - 470R  + LED to GND
\ ----------IN2 P2.2--[10   11]--P2.3 IN3
\ LP = TI Launchpad
\
\ P1.0 used as Input, later on as Analog Input 1
\ P1.1    RX and
\ P1.2    TX are used as the serial interface to the PC,
\              mostly via USBtoTTL
\ P1.3 used as S2, as on the TI Launchpad,
\              the internal resistor is enabled
\ P1.4 used as Input, later on as Analog Input 2
\ P1.5 used as Output, later on to output a frequency
\              with defined length
\ P1.6 Output, later on as Pulse Width Modulation output
\              - quasi D/A Output
\              resistor about 470 Ohms and LED to Ground
\ P1.7 Input S1, internal resistor enabled

\ P2.0 Input 0  internal resistor enabled, so open input means HIGH
\ P2.1 Input 1  internal resistor enabled, so open input means HIGH
\ P2.2 Input 2  internal resistor enabled, so open input means HIGH
\ P2.3 Input 3  internal resistor enabled, so open input means HIGH

\ P2.4 Output 0  resistor about 470 Ohms and LED to Ground
```

```
\ P2.5 Output 1  resistor about 470 Ohms and LED to Ground
\ P2.6 Output 2  resistor about 470 Ohms and LED to Ground
\ P2.7 Output 3  resistor about 470 Ohms and LED to Ground

\ One of the important issues to be solved here
\ was to use the FLASH memory of the MSP430 as an
\ EEPROM functionality needed for local programming,
\ this is an internal issue for later and can be skipped for now
\ The original Holtek Controller has 128 Bytes of EEPROM

\ 'EEROM' simulaton in flash memory  -- see the chapter further down


\ The Programming Model of this Minimum Processor
\ is simulated in Forth.
\ Remember: for simplicity this processor is used
\           as 4 bit, everything is in nibbles.
\           This is about the same processor
\          as in Burkhard Kainka's original design:

\ PC Program Counter limited to address memory locations 0 - 127,
\     00 to 7F in HEX
\ PG Page register 4 bit, combined with the 4 bit jump address
\     achieves the 256 ($100)
\ DL Delay register, a delay from 1ms to 60 sec can be programmed.
\ SK Skip register indicates a possible skip over instructions
\     based on comparisons
\     There are no conditional branches
\     - just these Conditional Skips for simplicity
\     Easy for beginners as the program code is relocatable
\     (address independent)

\ The main processor registers and other registers:

\ IN  4 bit input, when used reflects the status of the 4 Input lines
\ A   4 bit A register, somehow the central register,
\                         the ALU works with A register
\ B   4 bit B register
\ C   4 bit C register
\ D   4 bit D register
\ A1  4 bit Analog Input Channel 1
\ A2  4 bit Analog Input Channel 2
\ PW  4 bit Pulse Width Modulated Output, can used filtered
\                              as quasi analog output
```

```
\ OU  4 bit output register, 4 Output Pins will reflect
\                             the contents, LEDS display it


\ There are two options to program the program
\      for this simulated processor:
\      via the switches (and needes setting the IN bits
\      for page selection), or
\      control completely via the serial interface
\      - mostly to a PC, after enter q
\      so a more complex part of this program is used to
\      show the processor status
\      on the monitor
\      Display all of the variables in this processor,
\      here formatted differently

\  PC   PG DL SK    IN  A  B  C  D  A1 A2 PW  OU
\  x x  x  x  x     x   x  x  x  x  x  x  x   x

\ The next part of thei program is related to showing
\     how the FLASH Memory is used
\  as simulated EEPROM, so skip over this for now.



\ *** Let us start with an empty user flash ***

HEX   \ Just set for terminal IO and display,
      \   the options are HEX  and DECIMAL

\ membot 0000 + constant seg0 ; this did not work, see issues.
\ membot 0200 + constant seg1

\ PAD constant CACHE  \ PAD is already there in forth,
\    so we use it. Commented out here

1000 constant EE0    \ start address of info-d
1040 constant EE1    \ start address of info-c
0040 constant SEGSIZ \ segment size
0010 constant BLKSIZ \ bytes in block (alias "page" of MyCo)

variable SEG  \ holding segment number in use
variable BLK  \ holding block number
variable UPD  \ this variable shows if the cache has been updated
```

```
\ As we are simulating an existing system,
\   we use the same TPS example programs
\ 128 bytes of example programms = 8 pages -- page0 .. page7

HEX
IHERE
\ Page0
64 ic, 51 ic, 4E ic, 80 ic,
C3 ic, 98 ic, 82 ic, 95 ic,
4D ic, 80 ic, C3 ic, 9E ic,
82 ic, 9A ic, 4B ic, 81 ic,
\ Page1
C3 ic, 94 ic, 83 ic, 90 ic,
47 ic, 81 ic, C3 ic, 9A ic,
83 ic, 94 ic, 43 ic, 82 ic,
C3 ic, 90 ic, 84 ic, 90 ic,
\ Page2
11 ic, 28 ic, 18 ic, 28 ic,
34 ic, 71 ic, 54 ic, 59 ic,
26 ic, 34 ic, 69 ic, 54 ic,
59 ic, 26 ic, 34 ic, FF ic,
\ Page3
54 ic, CE ic, 71 ic, 33 ic,
22 ic, CC ic, 32 ic, 40 ic,
22 ic, 71 ic, 54 ic, CE ic,
34 ic, 39 ic, FF ic, FF ic,
\ Page4
86 ic, D0 ic, 40 ic, 71 ic,
54 ic, 23 ic, CD ic, 34 ic,
D8 ic, 40 ic, 54 ic, 3B ic,
FF ic, FF ic, FF ic, FF ic,
\ Page5
4F ic, 93 ic, 45 ic, 53 ic,
19 ic, 11 ic, 21 ic, 19 ic,
11 ic, 21 ic, 19 ic, 11 ic,
20 ic, B4 ic, 10 ic, E0 ic,
\ Page6
23 ic, CE ic, 32 ic, 23 ic,
CC ic, 31 ic, E0 ic, FF ic,
23 ic, CF ic, 32 ic, 23 ic,
CD ic, 31 ic, E0 ic, FF ic,
\ Page7
CC ic, 31 ic, 40 ic, 54 ic,
```

```
23 ic, CE ic, 32 ic, CF ic,
E0 ic, CC ic, 33 ic, 71 ic,
23 ic, CC ic, 31 ic, 3C ic,
ihere
constant EXEND
constant EX0


\ Now the real activity starts: The default programs above
\    are copied into the
\ 128 bytes of Program Area available for programming
\ and will show some demos,
\ using this code \ after a Reset.

HEX
: PRG0  \ --    \ copy the default progams to the
                \   simulated 'eeprom' area in FLASH
  ee0 segsiz flerase
  ee1 segsiz flerase
  ex0 ee0 exend ex0 - d->i  ;


\ The memory of the MSP430 will be rather fully used.
\   So, to save Program Space,
\ the 4 Bit Nibbles are packaged into 4 nibbles
\   to be one Variable of 16 bits.
\ This will save on RAM used, and is as well a programming exercise.



\ Juggling nibbles    mk0 (this shows how extensively
                           the code has been tested)
HEX
: 0! \ n adr -- \ store nibble 0 to value at address
  >r r@ @ FFF0 and swap F and + r> ! ;

: 1! \ n adr -- \ store nibble 1 to value at address
  >r r@ @ FF0F and swap F and 4 lshift + r> ! ;

: 2! \ n adr -- \ store nibble 2 to value at address
  >r r@ @ F0FF and swap F and 8 lshift + r> ! ;

: 3! \ n adr -- \ store nibble 3 to value at address
  >r r@ @ 0FFF and swap F and C lshift + r> ! ;
```

```
: 0@ \ adr - n \ fetch nibble 0 of value at address
  @ 000F and ;

: 1@ \ adr - n \ fetch nibble 1 of value at address
  @ 00F0 and 0004 rshift ;

: 2@ \ adr - n \ fetch nibble 2 of value at address
  @ 0F00 and 0008 rshift ;

: 3@ \ adr - n \ fetch nibble 3 of value at address
  @ F000 and 000C rshift ;


\ As a first step, we have to define and program the relevant IO Bits
\ of the chip as Input (with enabling internal pull-up resistor)
\ or as Output.
\ In this part of the program you can find the relevant memory mapped
\ addresses to
\   Set the IO functionality,
\   Read Input Data,
\   Write Output Data
\ Some of the possible internal MSP430 functions are rather complex,
\ so here
\ IO Bits are used as simple Input / Output only,
\ additional Forth Code later

HEX
: INITIO \ -- \ I/O initialisation of MyCo ports   mk0
\         mask            adr             op
\       76543210
[ bin ] 10011001 [ hex ] 0022 ( P1DIR ) cclr \ P1 INs
[ bin ] 01100110 [ hex ] 0022 ( P1DIR ) cset \ P1 OUTs
[ bin ] 10001000 [ hex ] 0024 ( P1IES ) cset \ falling edge detect
[ bin ] 00100000 [ hex ] 0026 ( P1SEL ) cset \ P1.5 sec func
                                             \ TA0.0 (FRQ)
[ bin ] 10001000 [ hex ] 0027 ( P1REN ) cset \ pullup selected
[ bin ] 10000000 [ hex ] P1             cset \ P1.7 pullup enabled
[ bin ] 00001111 [ hex ] 002A ( P2DIR ) cclr \ P2 INs
[ bin ] 11110000 [ hex ] 002A ( P2DIR ) cset \ P2 OUTs
[ bin ] 00001111 [ hex ] 002F ( P2REN ) cset \ P2 pullups selected
[ bin ] 00001111 [ hex ] P2             cset \ P2 pullups enabled
```

```
[ bin ] 11000000 [ hex ] 002E ( P2SEL ) cclr \ clear these bits
                                              \ to I/O

;    \ end of IO Setting Definition Word

INITIO      \ now execute the word INITIO

HEX    \ Set to HEX for some basic peripheral operations

: OUT! \ n -- \ write to output pins (nibble, 0004 LEDs)
              \ do NOT use c! word - this would reset the pull-ups!
  F0 p2 cclr 000F and 0004 lshift p2 cset ;

023 constant P1IFG    \ define a constant P1IFG

: S1?  080 P1IFG cget ;   \ -- f   \ set on edge event.
: S1-  080 P1IFG cclr ;   \ --    \ reset flag

: S2?  008 P1IFG cget ;   \ -- f   \ set on edge event.
: S2-  008 P1IFG cclr ;   \ --    \ reset flag

: IN@ \ -- n \ read digital input pins (nibble )
  P2 1- c@ 000F and ;



\ Now we are ready to define the simulated processor;
\ As explained before, the Registers are packed into 16 bit variables

\  SGPC PDSI ABCD 12WO
\  xxxx xxxx xxxx xxxx

HEX

variable SGPC     \ Segment(4 bit), PageCounter(4 bit)
                  \ and PC (2x 4 bit)

variable RTRN   \ ReTuRN address (copy of the SGPC before call happens)

variable PDSI     \ Page_Preset, Delay, Skip, Input

variable ABCD     \ registers A B C D

variable 12WO     \ ad1, ad2, pWm, out
```

```
\ LED display operations

: OUT> ( -- n ) 12wo 0@ ;        \ pull OUT nibble onto stack

: >OUT ( n -- ) 12wo 0! ;        \ push n to OUT nibble

: OUT.   \ n --  \               \ display n at OUT-LEDs,
                                 \ copy n to OUT-register
  dup out! >out ;


: ?  ( adr -- ) c@ . ;      \ define a Word to show the byte
                            \  ( 8 bits) at an address

: ?? ( adr -- ) @ u. ;      \ define a Word to show a cell
                            \ (16 bits) at address unsigned


\ Now we have to define the instructions
\ that this processor can execute
```

\ Define Instructions:

```
\ The first group of Instructions covers 0n -
\ n has the values of 00 to 0F
\ Tones are output by the MSP430G2553, 8Mhz DCO and SMCLK /2
```

```
HEX
\ 0n - set tone pitch n
\ output a square wave at P1.5 (pin 7)      mk0

: P15SEC  020 dup p1 1+ cset  026 cset ;  \ set P1.5 using TA0.0

: P15IO   020 026 cclr  020 041 cclr ;    \ set p1.5 as GPIO

: TON-  zero 0160 ! p15io ;  \ stop timer

: TON+ \ n --                  \ start timer-A with interval n
  p15sec     \ init pin
  0080  0162 !  \ CCTL0  set timer output mode
  ( n ) 0172 !  \ CCR0   set interval
  0254  0160 !  \ CTL    start timer clock, mode and divider
  ;

\ --> intermediate-stage-0.txt
\ up to here can be programmed using the intermediate-stage-0.txt file


DECIMAL       \ MIDI Tones B3 to B5, 2 Octaves; pitch list.   mk0
: 00  ton- ;
: 01  7962 ton+ ; \ B3
: 02  7515 ton+ ; \ C4
: 03  6695 ton+ ; \ D4
: 04  5965 ton+ ; \ E4
: 05  5630 ton+ ; \ F4
: 06  5016 ton+ ; \ G4
: 07  4469 ton+ ; \ A4
: 08  3981 ton+ ; \ B4
: 09  3758 ton+ ; \ C5
: 0A  3348 ton+ ; \ D5
: 0B  2983 ton+ ; \ E5
: 0C  2815 ton+ ; \ F5
: 0D  2508 ton+ ; \ G5
: 0E  2235 ton+ ; \ A5
: 0F  1991 ton+ ; \ B5

\ The next group of Instructions covers 1n - 10 to 1F,
```

```
\ just stores a hex number into the Output register,
\ no other register affected
```

\ 1n - Load Out with number n \ mk1

```
HEX
: 10 0000 out. ;
: 11 0001 out. ;
: 12 0002 out. ;
: 13 0003 out. ;
: 14 0004 out. ;
: 15 0005 out. ;
: 16 0006 out. ;
: 17 0007 out. ;
: 18 0008 out. ;
: 19 0009 out. ;
: 1A 000A out. ;
: 1B 000B out. ;
: 1C 000C out. ;
: 1D 000D out. ;
: 1E 000E out. ;
: 1F 000F out. ;
```

\ 2n - Load the Delay Register with a number from 0-F mk1

```
DECIMAL
: DLY ( n -- ) PDSI 2! ;
: SEC ( n -- ) 0000 DO 1000 ms LOOP ;

: 20 0000 dly 1ms ;
: 21 0001 dly 0002 ms ;
: 22 0002 dly 0005 ms ;
: 23 0003 dly 0010 ms ;
: 24 0004 dly 0020 ms ;
: 25 0005 dly 0050 ms ;
: 26 0006 dly 0100 ms ;
: 27 0007 dly 0200 ms ;
: 28 0008 dly 0500 ms ;
: 29 0009 dly 0001 sec ;
: 2A 0010 dly 0002 sec ;
: 2B 0011 dly 0005 sec ;
: 2C 0012 dly 0010 sec ;
: 2D 0013 dly 0020 sec ;
: 2E 0014 dly 0030 sec ;
: 2F 0015 dly 0060 sec ;
```

```
\ 3n -  Instruction to Jump back 0 to F locations
\       of the current program counter PC = PC-n \ mk1

HEX
: JB \ n --    \ subtract n from program counter
  invert SGPC +! ;
: 30 0000 jb ;
: 31 0001 jb ;
: 32 0002 jb ;
: 33 0003 jb ;
: 34 0004 jb ;
: 35 0005 jb ;
: 36 0006 jb ;
: 37 0007 jb ;
: 38 0008 jb ;
: 39 0009 jb ;
: 3A 000A jb ;
: 3B 000B jb ;
: 3C 000C jb ;
: 3D 000D jb ;
: 3E 000E jb ;
: 3F 000F jb ;

\ 4n - Instruction to load register A with a number n  k1
HEX
: NTOA ( n -- ) abcd 3! ; \ A<=N
: 40 0000 NTOA ;
: 41 0001 NTOA ;
: 42 0002 NTOA ;
: 43 0003 NTOA ;
: 44 0004 NTOA ;
: 45 0005 NTOA ;
: 46 0006 NTOA ;
: 47 0007 NTOA ;
: 48 0008 NTOA ;
: 49 0009 NTOA ;
: 4A 000A NTOA ;
: 4B 000B NTOA ;
: 4C 000C NTOA ;
: 4D 000D NTOA ;
: 4E 000E NTOA ;
: 4F 000F NTOA ;
```

```
\ 5n -  Instruction, Transfer register A
\                     to other locations,
\                     nibble or bit \   mk0
\                     including starting the PWM activity

HEX
: P16IO
  0040 0022 cset    \ P1DIR   P1.6 out
  0040 0026 cclr    \ P1SEL   P1.6 GPIO
  ;

: P16SEL
  0040 0022 cset    \ P1DIR   P1.6 out
  0040 0026 cset    \ P1SEL   P1.6 select second function
  ;

: PWM-
  zero 160 !  \ TA0CTL   stop timer
  p16io 0040 0021 cclr ; \ set p1.6 I/O and clear p1.6

: PWM+  \ n --  \ init and start PWM at P1.6
  01F4 0172 !   \ TA0CCR0    set period 16KHz at 8MHZ DCO
  00E0 0164 !   \ TA0CCTL1   set output mode
       0174 !   \ TA0CCR1    set pulsewidth
  0210 0160 !   \ TA0CTL     set timer mode and run
  ;

: PWM!  \ n --   \ set PWM at P1.6 with register A
  dup 0= IF drop pwm-
  ELSE 001F * pwm+ p16sel THEN ;

: 50 ; \ nc
: 51 abcd 3@ abcd 2! ; \ B<=A
: 52 abcd 3@ abcd 1! ; \ C<=A
: 53 abcd 3@ abcd 0! ; \ D<=A
: 54 abcd 3@ 12wo 0! ; \ OUT<=A
: 55 abcd 3@ 001 and  out> or 12wo 0! ;            \ OUT.0<=A.0
: 56 abcd 3@ 001 and  001 lshift out> or 12wo 0! ; \ OUT.1<=A.0
: 57 abcd 3@ 001 and  002 lshift out> or 12wo 0! ; \ OUT.2<=A.0
: 58 abcd 3@ 001 and  003 lshift out> or 12wo 0! ; \ OUT.4<=A.0
: 59 abcd 3@ dup 12wo 1! pwm! ; \ PWM<=A   mk0
: 5A ; \ nc
: 5B ; \ nc
: 5C ; \ nc
```

```
: 5D ; \ nc
: 5E ; \ nc
: 5F ; \ nc

\  For now we just emulate the original TPS version, 128 bytes,
\       but later on, there might be double program memory size from 128
to 256
```

\ 6n - Instruction, Transfer nibbles from other locations to register A \   mk0

```
BIN
: GETIN  \ move digital input port pin values to IN register nibbles
  in@ PDSI 0! ;

: 60 ; \ nc
: 61 abcd 2@ abcd 3! ; \ A<=B
: 62 abcd 1@ abcd 3! ; \ A<=C
: 63 abcd 0@ abcd 3! ; \ A<=D
: 64 getin pdsi 0@ abcd 3! ; \ A<=IN
: 65 getin pdsi 0@ 0001 and abcd 3@ or abcd 3! ; \ A.0<=IN.0
: 66 getin pdsi 0@ 0010 and abcd 3@ or abcd 3! ; \ A.0<=IN.1
: 67 getin pdsi 0@ 0100 and abcd 3@ or abcd 3! ; \ A.0<=IN.2
: 68 getin pdsi 0@ 1000 and abcd 3@ or abcd 3! ; \ A.0<=IN.3
: 69 ; \ nc
: 6A ; \ nc
: 6B ; \ nc
: 6C ; \ nc
: 6D ; \ nc
: 6E ; \ nc
: 6F ; \ nc
```

```
\ 7n -  Instruction - maths and logic \   mk0
HEX

: 70 ; \ nc
: 71 abcd 3@ 1+ abcd 3! ;           \ A<=A+1
: 72 abcd 3@ 1- abcd 3! ;           \ A<=A-1
: 73 abcd 3@ abcd 2@ + abcd 3! ;    \ A<=A+B
: 74 abcd 3@ abcd 2@ - abcd 3! ;    \ A<=A-B
: 75 abcd 3@ abcd 2@ * abcd 3! ;    \ A<=A*B
: 76 abcd 3@ abcd 2@ / abcd 3! ;    \ A<=A/B
: 77 abcd 3@ abcd 2@ and abcd 3! ; \ A=(A AND B)
: 78 abcd 3@ abcd 2@ or abcd 3! ;  \ A<=(A OR B)
: 79 abcd 3@ abcd 2@ xor abcd 3! ; \ A<=(A XOR B)
: 7A abcd 3@ invert abcd 3! ;       \ A<=notA
: 7B ; \ nop
: 7C ; \ nop
: 7D ; \ nop
: 7E ; \ nop
: 7F ; \ nop

\ 8n -  Instruction - Set the Page Register \   mk1
\                         This is used to jump more then 16 locations
HEX
: LDPGE \ n --   \ store n as page preset.
  PDSI 3! ;

: 80 0000 ldpge ;
: 81 0001 ldpge ;
: 82 0002 ldpge ;
: 83 0003 ldpge ;
: 84 0004 ldpge ;
: 85 0005 ldpge ;
: 86 0006 ldpge ;
: 87 0007 ldpge ;
: 88 ; \ nc
: 89 ; \ nc
: 8A ; \ nc
: 8B ; \ nc
: 8C ; \ nc
: 8D ; \ nc
: 8E ; \ nc
: 8F ; \ nc
\ This will be extended to work on 256 bytes later,
\ double the original
```

```
\ 9n -  Instruction - Jump to any location,
\                          page register has to be set first \   mk1

HEX
: JMP       \ n --    \ jump to preset page at addr n.
  1-        \ do n-1 because counter is incremented in nexi afterwards.
  SGPC 0!  \ set program counter C nibble to n.
  PDSI 3@ 008 or  PDSI 3!  ;  \ set page preset flag.

: 90 0000 jmp ;
: 91 0001 jmp ;
: 92 0002 jmp ;
: 93 0003 jmp ;
: 94 0004 jmp ;
: 95 0005 jmp ;
: 96 0006 jmp ;
: 97 0007 jmp ;
: 98 0008 jmp ;
: 99 0009 jmp ;
: 9A 000A jmp ;
: 9B 000B jmp ;
: 9C 000C jmp ;
: 9D 000D jmp ;
: 9E 000E jmp ;
: 9F 000F jmp ;

\ An -  Instruction -  Multiply register C * n \   mk0
HEX
: C* ( n -- ) abcd 1@ * abcd 1! ;

: A0 0000 c* ;
: A1 0001 c* ;
: A2 0002 c* ;
: A3 0003 c* ;
: A4 0004 c* ;
: A5 0005 c* ;
: A6 0006 c* ;
: A7 0007 c* ;
: A8 0008 c* ;
: A9 0009 c* ;
: AA 000A c* ;
: AB 000B c* ;
: AC 000C c* ;
: AD 000D c* ;
```

```
: AE 000E c* ;
: AF 000F c* ;
```

\ Bn - Instruction - Multiply register D * n \ mk0

```
HEX
: D* ( n -- ) abcd 0@ * abcd 0! ;

: B0 0000 d* ;
: B1 0001 d* ;
: B2 0002 d* ;
: B3 0003 d* ;
: B4 0004 d* ;
: B5 0005 d* ;
: B6 0006 d* ;
: B7 0007 d* ;
: B8 0008 d* ;
: B9 0009 d* ;
: BA 000A d* ;
: BB 000B d* ;
: BC 000C d* ;
: BD 000D d* ;
: BE 000E d* ;
: BF 000F d* ;
```

\ Cn - Instructions - used to generate possible Skips \ mk1

```
HEX
: NEXI        \ --      \ proceed to next instruction
  1 sgpc +!             \ increment address
  pdsi 3@ 007 > IF
    pdsi 3@ 007 and   dup sgpc 1! pdsi 3!
  THEN ;
: SKIP  \ f --          \ if f is true, skip.
  IF NEXI THEN ;

: C0 ;
: C1 abcd 3@ abcd 2@ > skip ; \ A>B
: C2 abcd 3@ abcd 2@ < skip ; \ A<B
: C3 abcd 3@ abcd 2@ = skip ; \ A=B
BIN
: C4 pdsi 0@ 0001 and 0001 = skip ; \ IN.0=1
```

```
: C5 pdsi 0@ 0010 and 0010 = skip ; \ IN.1=1
: C6 pdsi 0@ 0100 and 0100 = skip ; \ IN.2=1
: C7 pdsi 0@ 1000 and 1000 = skip ; \ IN.3=1
: C8 pdsi 0@ 0001 and 0= skip ; \ IN.0=0
: C9 pdsi 0@ 0010 and 0= skip ; \ IN.1=0
: CA pdsi 0@ 0100 and 0= skip ; \ IN.2=0
: CB pdsi 0@ 1000 and 0= skip ; \ IN.3=0
HEX
: CC s1? invert skip s1- ; \ S1=0
: CD s2? invert skip s2- ; \ S2=0
: CE s1? skip s1- ; \ S1=1
: CF s2? skip s2- ; \ S2=1
```

\ Dn - Instruction - Call a Subroutine

```
\                    - only one allowed, no nesting yet
\                                                              mk0
HEX
: CALL \ n --      \ Save return address, then call subroutine n in
preset page.
  NEXI            \ current program counter + 1 is return address,
  SGPC @ RTRN !   \ save it.
  jmp  ;          \ jump to n in preset page.

: D0 0000 call ;
: D1 0001 call ;
: D2 0002 call ;
: D3 0003 call ;
: D4 0004 call ;
: D5 0005 call ;
: D6 0006 call ;
: D7 0007 call ;
: D8 0008 call ;
: D9 0009 call ;
: DA 000A call ;
: DB 000B call ;
: DC 000C call ;
: DD 000D call ;
: DE 000E call ;
: DF 000F call ;
```

```
\ En -  Instruction - Return from Subroutine \   mk0
: E0  \ --   \ copy RETN address to SGPC.
  rtrn @ sgpc !  sgpc 1@ pdsi 3! ;
\ E1..EF are not assigned



\ F0..FF are not assigned yet
\ Just for reloading the initial EEPROM Code
\ when FF FF found at address 0 and 1

\ --> intermediate-stage-1.txt




\ -----------------------------------------------------------

\ RUN and Debug MyCo programs

\ RUN starting at zero page.
HEX
: NOINDI  \ --  \ indicator LED off
  40 59 ;

: INIT   \ --   \ initialisation of the environment
  SGPC 005 cells 000 fill  \ clr registers,
  ee0 SGPC !               \ set start address of programs,
  initio hex               \ set all I/O and number base,
  ee0 @ FFFF = IF prg0 THEN   \ check for default program.
  noindi zero out. ;       \  "GUI" off


: OP@ \ -- n \ get opcode
  SGPC @ c@ ;

: EVAL  \ n -- \ evaluate instruction
  <# zero # # #> evaluate ;

: EXOP  \ --   \ execute opcode
  op@ eval nexi ;
```

```
: RUN  \ --    \ run a programm.
  init s1- s2-
  BEGIN
  exop
  key? s2? s1? or or UNTIL  \ enter Forth on any key
  s2? s1? or IF s1- s2- ELSE key drop THEN
  zero out. ;
```

\ LOG program step by step.

```
HEX
: 4#    \ n --   \ display 4 digits unsigned
  <# zero # # # # #> TYPE SPACE ;
: "RNM \ --  \ type register names
  ." SGPC UUOP RTRN PDSI ABCD 12WO" ;
: .RGS \ -- \ dump registers
  base @ >r hex
  SGPC @ 4#
  op@    4#
  rtrn @ 4#
  pdsi @ 4#
  abcd @ 4#
  12wo @ 4#
  r> base ! ;

: LOG   \ --   \ use space bar to log program      mk0
  init cr  "rnm
  BEGIN cr .rgs
  key 020 = WHILE exop REPEAT ; \ enter Forth on any key but blank


\ Note: Use VT100 terminal emulator.
\       For example 4e4th IDE or Teraterm
```

\ Single STEP through the entire program and dump

```
HEX
: 2#    \ n --   \ display 2 digits unsigned
  <# zero # # #> TYPE SPACE ;
```

```
: PMAP  \ --   \ print program memory map
  zero 003 at-xy   \ start position
  004 spaces 010 zero DO i 2# space LOOP cr  \ print horizontal ruler
  008 zero DO cr i 2#  \ print vertical ruler, 8 pages
  010 zero DO
  ee0 i j 010 * + + c@
  space 2#
  LOOP LOOP ;

: POS   \ --   \ cursor pointing at code in program dump.
  sgpc 0@ 004 * 004 +
  sgpc 1@ 005 +
  at-xy ;

: STEP  \ --  \ use space bar to single step
\               through program                         mk0
  init page "rnm pmap
  BEGIN 000 001 at-xy .rgs
  pos  key 020 = \ stop loop, enter Forth on any key but blank
  WHILE exop REPEAT  000 00D at-xy ;

\ Footnote: PAGE is a standard Forth Word.
\ It is an alias for 'clear screen'.
\ Do not mix up with the MyCo program page register.


\ --> intermediate-stage-2.txt
```

\ ---

\ Simulate 'EEPROM' using INFO-C and -D flash memory.

```
\ Note:
\ The idea is to have a cache, edit there, and flush it back
\ to mass storage when done.

\ Have a cache in 4e4th - where is RAM for it?
\ An info segment is 64 bytes.
\ Address range is $1000 .. $107F
\ That is 128 bytes or 8 blocks of 16 bytes each.
\ Forth scratch PAD is 80 bytes.
\ PAD is not used inside of Forth.
\ So a segment buffer, the cache, may be build in PAD area.
```

```
\ Only whole segments of flash can be written.
\ So get segment into cache, edit block there,
\ and flush back when done or a block in the other segment is used.



\ Naming memory segments, cache, its variables and constants:

HEX
: wipecache  \ -- \ fill cache with zeros, set variables...
  pad segsiz 0 fill
  0 upd !  FFFF blk !  0 seg !  ;

: update  \ --  \ mark the cache as updated
  FFFF upd ! ;
```

\ Examine 'eeprom' and cache

```
: ?EE   \ --  \ dump 'eeprom' to screen (testing utility)  ok
  base @
  hex ee0 segsiz 2* dump
  base ! ;

: ?CA  \ dump cache
  base @  cr blk ?  upd ?
  hex pad segsiz dump
  base ! ;
```

\ move 'eeprom' segments to cache and back

```
: eeadr   \ n -- adr \ calculate address of segment
  1 and   \ n = 0..1  only
  segsiz * ee0 + ;

: cache  \ n -- \   copy info segment from adr to cache   ok
  eeadr pad segsiz move ;

: backup  \ n -- \ copy cache back to segment   ok
  eeadr >r                   \ make addr a local variable
  r@ segsiz flerase  \ clear flash segment
  pad r> segsiz d->i ; \ move data to instruction memory (flash)
```

```
: FLUSH  \ --   \ if updated copy pad to segment   ok
  upd @ IF seg @ backup THEN ;
```

\ Move block to cache

```
: blkadr  \ n -- adr \ calculate address of block in cache
  3 and   \ n = 0..3  only
  blksiz * pad +  ;

: BLOCK \ n -- adr \ cache block n
  dup  blk @ = IF blkadr exit THEN  \ block is in cache already.
  flush
  7 and blk !    \ 0..7 blocks only
  blk @ 3 >   1 and   seg !  \ calculate segment
  seg @ cache    \ get segment
  0 upd !        \ mark as unchanged
  blk @ blkadr ; \ put block address on stack
```

\ Edit items in a block

```
HEX
: dolist \ adr -- \ print a block
  dup blksiz + swap
  DO i c@ 2# LOOP ;

: ruler \ -- \    print a block ruler
  blksiz 0 DO i 2# LOOP ;

: LIST \ n --  \ list block n to screen
  cr ruler
  cr block dolist ;

: >>  \ b n -- \  poke byte and show result.
  blk @ blkadr + c!   \ write byre b into n-th position
                      \ of current block in cache
  blk @ list update ;
```

```
\ prg0 ee?  \ test fill info segments C and D.


\ --> intermediate-stage-3.txt



\ -----------------------------------------------------------
\ EDIT a Page of memory using S1 and S2 on MyCo-board,
\ no serial interface used.
\ Edit in cache, and when done save to 'eeprom'.

\ select page
\ start at position zero in page
\ display address
\ edit high nibble
\ edit low nibble
\ autoincrement position in page
\ flush if done
\ select byte


HEX
\ more switch conditions
: S1?? \ -- f   \ true if S1 is down
  080 020 cget  0= ;
: S2?? \ -- f   \ true if S2 is down
  008 020 cget  0= ;
: S1DOWN? \ -- f  \ true if S1 is held down
  s1?? s1?? and s1?? and ;   \ debouncing
: S2DOWN? \ -- f  \ true if S2 is held down
  s2?? s2?? and s2?? and ;   \ debouncing
: SWAIT \ -- \ wait till switch is pressed
  s1- s2- BEGIN s2? s1? or UNTIL
  29 ;  \ 1s delay - time to press the other switch too.
  \ this works because pressing a switch is hardware detected
  \ by it's falling edge


\ more indicator LED "GUI"  (PWM driven LED)
: BRIGHT \ --  \ bright green LED indicating upper nibble
  4F 59 ;
```

```
: DIMMED \ --  \ dimmed green LED indicating lower nibble
  41 59 ;
: SHADED \ --  \ shaded green LED indicating lower nibble
  44 59 ;
: setpwm \ n -- \ set pwm to n  (n=0..F)
  0040 + eval 59   23 ( delay ) ;
: SWELL  \ --
  0010 0006 DO i setpwm     LOOP
  0001 000F DO i setpwm -1 +LOOP
  0006 0000 DO i setpwm     LOOP
  ;
```

\ edit both nibbles in a byte

```
: INC-OUT \  increment OUT
  out> 1+ out.  ;
: EDOUT \ n -- n' \ edit nibble n using S1 to inc and S2 to exit
  s1- s2- out.
  BEGIN  \ single step or hold down S1 to increment n
  s1down?
  IF inc-out   27 ( delay ) THEN
  s2? UNTIL
  s1- s2-  \ clear flags
  out> ;   \ put n' on stack
: EDHI   \ adr -- \ edit nibble-1 in variable at address
  bright
  >r
  r@ 1@ edout r> 1! ;
: EDLO   \ adr -- \ edit nibble-0 in variable at address
  dimmed
  >r
  r@ 0@ edout r> 0! ;
: EDC \ adr --  \ edit byte at address of cache
  sgpc !             \ save addr to cache pointer
  sgpc @ c@ abcd c! \ get byte to abcd
  noindi 28          \ delay
  abcd edhi          \ set new value in abcd nibble c
  noindi 28
  abcd edlo          \ set new value in abcd nibble d
  sgpc @ c@  abcd c@ <>    \ if altered ...
  IF abcd c@  sgpc @ c! update THEN ;  \ store and set update flag

: EDBYTE \ -- \ edit byte at current position in current page
  blk @ blkadr rtrn 0@ +   edc ;
```

```
: SELPAGE \ -- \ select page using
\                S1 to inc and S2 to exit
  swell swell swell
  zero edout block drop  \ make SELPAGE = BLOCK in forth
  noindi ;

: SELPOS \ --  \ select position in page
  rtrn 0@ edout rtrn 0! ;
  \ we use variable RTRN as pointer to byte in page

: EDPAGE \ -- \ edit current page ( = block number )
  zero rtrn !  \ start with byte zero
  BEGIN
  swell swell  rtrn 0@ out.
  swait s1? s2? and 0= WHILE
  s2down? IF swell selpos THEN  \ select position in page
\                                 if S2 is held down
  edbyte                        \ edit byte at selected position
  rtrn 0@ 1+ rtrn 0!            \ increment position
  REPEAT
  flush noindi zero out.
  s1- s2- ;

: SEDIT \ --   \ edit MyCo program page using S2 and S1
  selpage edpage ;

\ --> intermediate-stage-4.txt



\ -----------------------------------------------------------
\ MyCo
\ User interface of MyCo:
\ Buttons S1 and S2, 4 LEDs, reset button.



HEX
: BLINK  \  blink 4 LEDs to indicate wait state  mk
  000f out. 28  \ 500 ms delay
```

```
  zero out. 28  ;

: MAIN
  blink
  s1? IF run   exit THEN   \ press S1 to run program
  s2? IF sedit exit THEN   \ press S2 to enter S1S2 edit mode
  ;

: Q?  \ -- f   \ quit - press q to leave MyCo
  key? if key 0071 ( q ) = else zero then ;

: MYCO
  28                     \ 500 ms delay
  ee0 @ IF prg0 THEN   \ check, load default program
  init s1- s2-  noindi \ initialisation
  BEGIN main Q? UNTIL ." Forth "  ;  \ mk0

\ --> intermediate-stage-5.txt

\ ' myco app !
\ save

\ decimal mem u.


\ todo ***
\ verify opcodes

( finis )
```

MyCo Control Instructions

Michael Kalus/ Juergen Pintaske
Version 0.9.1 4e4th Version 2015_04_04

Switching on Power or Reset starts MyCo program.
The 4 LEDs at OUT will flash. The indicator LED (PWM LED) is switched off.

Idle State - MyCo is ready and waiting for an input either via S1 / S2 or via the keyboard.

S1 - Switch pressed - MyCo program starts
S2 - Switch pressed - MyCo switches ino Programming Mode
– no connection to thePC required
'q' - Entered on Terminal - 4e4th Forth starts (Only works if keyboard is connected / MyCo in dle State)

- To Run a Program already intalled-
In Idle State press S1. MyCo will then enters the Program Run Mode. MyCo programs always start at page 0 address $00. To terminate a running MyCo program: press S1 or S2 key - or any key on the keyboard.

- Show the Program Flow –

A)-using the 4 LEDs ---
To view the program steps from the outside, a MyCo program has to make outputs to the 4 LEDs, otherwise nothing is visible. Additional LED test output instructions can be added for debugging. Later replaced by NOPs. Extensions: Use a volt meter to check the levels at IN and OUT and to watch – or a multimeter or an oscilloscope.

B) Using Forth and the Serial Interface--- Using the additional options
The MyCo Program runs using the Interactive Programming Language Forth. There are 3 additional services provided in this mode in order to test the program flow step by step. Using the space bar on the keyboard, you step through the whole program. The status of all registers and other IO are shown:

LOG writes the MyCo program sequence step by step. Press the space bar to step through the whole program.

Register contents, state at Input Port and Output Port will be displayed.

STEP displays the entire contents of the MyCo memory in one go. Here as well, step through the whole program by pressing the space bar. Registers and Ports are displayed step by step.
So you see exactly at which point of the program you are and which activity has been executed (single stepping).

RUN starts the MyCo Program in Flash memory. In this way the effects on periphery can be seen. Pressing any key on the keyboard stops the MyCo program execution, and you come back to the Forth Operating System level.

- Programming –

Press S2 when in Idle State. MyCo status changes into the Programming Mode. Programming of a MyCo program is done code block by block (page), then each block byte by byte, and each byte nibble by nibble. To start, first the target page must be selected that will be processed.

- Select Page -

Indicator LED flashes 3 times. Using S1, one of 8 pages can be selected. Default page is page-0. Continue using S2.

- Select Bytes -

By repeatedly pressing S2 one program byte after the other can be displayed. In This way all bytes of the selected page can be inspected, contents will be shown via the 4 LEDs. Here each byte is shown in three steps.

View Memory Contents - Press S2 repeatedly

Step	Indicator LED (PWM)	Description of 4 LED display
1	2x flashing in medium bright	byte address within the page
2	from off -> to bright	high nibble
3	from off-> to dim	low nibble

The **Read/Modify Modus** starts at byte address zero, so the 4 LEDs are thus first all switched off.
Press S2 and the Hi-nibble of the byte is displayed.
S2 again, and the Lo nibble is displayed.
Press again S2, and MyCo begins another 3-step display, now at byte address +1
After 16 bytes the procedure starts again at byte 0, MyCo stays on same page (wrap around).

- Edit a Nibble - In Step_2 or Step_3 the contents of a nibble can increment by pressing S1. After $F the value is back to zero. You can step through the value as often as needed. End of nibble change input with S2.

- Select Byte Start Address – If in step_1 button S2 is kept pressed, MyCo jumps into Start Address Select. Indicator LED flashes 1x, LEDs show the current byte address, incremented via S1. If new address set, S2 changes mode back to 3 step display from the new adddress.

- End Editing and Transfer and Program into FLASH Memory - Press both buttons, S2 + S1 simultaneously;
Back to IDLE Mode, 4 LEDs flash, at the same time edited page is written back to Flash memory.
MyCo returns to IDLE MODE. In this case, changes to the nibbles are transferred to the 'eeprom'.

11 - ATTiny84 as TPS PLC

From Willie's website

http://wkla.no-ip.biz/ArduinoWiki/doku.php?id=arduino:arduinosps:attiny
My TPS simulator includes as well as target the ATtiny84 variant. To use this version, the Arduino IDE must contain the ATtiny Core. In the Arduino IDE you must first add an additional board manager URL in the preferences.
http://drazzy.com/package_drazzy.com_index.json
Then you can install the ATtinyCore by Spance Konde and then select the ATtiny24 / 44/ 84 board in the board selection area. It is also important to put the pin mapping on COunterClockWise (old ATtiny Core) Now you can recompile the TPS, and program the generated code version into the Tiny with an ISP programmer.

The following assignment of the ATTiny pins to the TPS inputs / outputs applies:

SPS Connections	Arduino related	Attiny84 Pins
Din1, 2, 3, 4	D10, 9, 8, 7	13, 12, 11, 10
Dout1, 2, 3, 4	D6, 5, 4, 1	9, 8, 7, 3
PWM1, 2	D2, 3	5, 6
Servo1, 2	D2, 3	5, 6
ADC1, 2	A0, A1	13, 12
RC1,2	D9, D10	12, 13
SW_PRG	D0	2
SW_SEL	D8	11

14 Pin Chip TOP View

	Plus	**Pin1**	Pin14	**Ground**		
	SW_PRG	Pin2	Pin13	ADC1	RC2	Din1
Dout4		Pin3	Pin12	ADC2	RC1	Din2
	RESET	Pin4	Pin11	**SW_SEL**		Din3
Servo1	PWM1	Pin5	Pin10			Din4
Servo2	PWM2	Pin6	Pin9	Dout1		
Dout3		Pin7	Pin8	Dout2		

Unfortunately, dual use of pins on the ATtiny can not be avoided, because there are only 11 pins left after deducting the power supply and reset pin. Thus, e.g. Servo and PWM can not be used simultaneously. The SEL switch is on the input 3 pin. And the two ADC inputs occupy the digital inputs D1 and D2. Pin 11 of the ATtiny is needed for the reset. And the ATtiny is operated with internal clock at 8MHz. Here's the current Arduino to Pin assignment of the ATtiny core:

A A C D E F G H I K

Ground	notcon2	1
Plus	Ground	2
SW_PRG	in1	3
out4	in2	4
RESET	in3	5
PWM1	in4	6
PWM2	out1	7
out3	out2	8
	LED4	9
		10
	LED3	11
		12
	LED2	13
		14
	LED1	15
		16
	notcon1	17

Attiny84 Board - parts on solderless breadboard

Holtek on Breadboard / ATTINY84 TPS waiting for chip delivery

12 - Is Programming it really so difficult?

Let's look at this programming stuff from a completely different angle. It seems to be all so technical and only for the specialists.
WRONG.

We all do it every day.
The major part of this MyCo Programming Stuff we do every day, let's get started:

First we have to understand the Number Systems of Humans and Computers.

Decimal:

We are all used to the **decimal system**. 10 different numbers. Why is it a decimal system? Well, look at your fingers – you have (normally) 10. We count from 0, 1, 2, 3, 4, 5, 6, 7, 8 9. We have then exhausted our numbers, do an overflow to 1 0 – an additional number 1 in front of our counting, and continue counting with 11, 12, and so on, until we come to the next overflow – from 99 to 1 00 – now 3 digits and so on.

Binary:

Computers do not use 10 states of 0 to 9 as in decimal, they only have two states.
They can only distinguish 0 and 1 or on and off – so 2 options rather than the 10 we are used to. Hence the name Binary System. But it works as well.
You use the same overflow as in a decimal system. The number in brackets here is the number in decimal).
Start with 0 (0) , then the next one which is 1 (1) .
Now we have exhausted the different values possible and have to have the same overflow as in our decimal system:
And as consequence 0 (1) , leads to 1 (1) and next 10 (2) and 11 (3),
and next again we have to generate an overflow and from 11 (3) to 100 (4), 101 (5), 110 (6), 111 (7),
then later 1000 (8), 1001 (9), 1010 (10), 1011 (11), 1100 (12), 1101 (13), 1110 (14) 1111 (15) and again there would be an overflow to 1 0000 (16).
This now leads to 5 number positions, but our system here is limited to 4 positions – a 4 bit system.
In binary, numbers will end up with rather long strings of 0s and 1s.

We could divide up the long strings into blocks of 4 bits – and would, as shown above, have in each block 16 possibilities. There is the unusual situation, that the "translated" 4 bit binary number block can consist of 1 (0 to 9) or 2 digits (10 ..15).

It was decided, that 0 to 9 stay as is, and the rest is replaced by A (10) B(11) C (12) D(13) E(14) F (15). As there are now 16 "numbers", this system is called hexadecimal.

The table further down shows long strings of numbers – here up to 32 bits, and you see the numbers divided up unto 8 4-bit blocks – shorter to write for the same number in hexadecimal.

This table shows on the left the decimal representation of the long sequence of a 1 plus many 0s. Numbers are rounded in some areas, so you can memorize some examples more easily. Translated into hexadecimal, the numbers would be:
1 2 4 8   10 20 40 80   100 200 400 800   1000 2000 4000 8000 and so on.

We will stay in our system here within the 4 bits marked, so our possible numbers are as stated before in binary, in brackets as in decimal until 9, and the last 6 in decimal / hexadecimal:
0 (0)   1 (1)   10 (2)   11 (3)   100 (4)   101 (5)   110 (6)   111 (7)
1000 (8)   1001 (9)   1010 (10/A)   1011 (11/B)   1100 (12/C)   1101 (13/D)   1110 (14/E)   1111 (15/F)

Size / Bits	31	30	29	28	27	26	25	24	23	22	21	20	19	18	17	16	15	14	13	12	11	10	9	8	7	6	5	4	3	2	1	0
1																																1
2																															1	
4																														1		
8																													1			
16																												1				
32																											1					
64																										1						
128																									1							
256																								1								
512																							1									
(1000) 1024																						1										
2 000																					1											
4 000																				1												
8 000																			1													
16 000																		1														
32 000																	1															
64 000																1																
128 000															1																	
256 000														1																		
512 000													1																			
(1 000 000)												1																				
2 000 000											1																					
4 000 000										1																						
8 000 000									1																							
16 000 000								1																								
32 000 000							1																									
64 000 000						1																										
128 000 000					1																											
256 000 000				1																												
512 000 000			1																													
1000 000 000		1																														
2 000 000 000	1																															
4 000 000 000	1	1	1	1	1	1	1	1	1	1	1	1	1	1	1	1	1	1	1	1	1	1	1	1	1	1	1	1	1	1	1	1

The full width of this table uses 32 different bits like in a 32 bit computer – and to compare the range covered to something in the real world:

this range of numbers is good enough to give every second person on this planet a unique number – about 8 billion people on earth soon.

We have covered now, very roughly, the three main number systems we use: decimal, hexadecimal and binary; the computer only uses binary – the rest is for our better understanding and for communicating with the computer.

With this as a basis, we can start looking at programming – and compare it with everyday tasks.

INPUT | REGISTER A | ALU | REGISTER B | REGISTER C | REGISTER D | DELAY | OUT

INPUT 1
INPUT 2
INPUT 3
INPUT 4

OUTPUT 1
OUTPUT 2
OUTPUT 3
OUTPUT 4

To work through our recipee / program, we use a system as shown here. We can blow it up and put it on the table, see picture. Add them up – there are 1 2 4 and 8 mug blocks – together the maximum number of 15 we will work with here.

We have mainly 8 blocks in our processor (number 9 PAGE) we leave for later:

An Input Block, where data (or here units of anything) enter the unit
Registers A, B , C and D, where we can store numbers of units
Processing of Numbers is done in the ALU block (Arithmetic and Logic Unit)
Add and subtract (Maths)
We can compare them (Logic) and use the result for decisions
A Timer Block DELAY, where the computer takes a predefined break
The Output block, where the results leave our processor.

The same blocks as in the small processor picture, here now as seperate A4 sheets in the picture. There you can then move Stick-It notes around.
The actual processor function of each page is highlighted on the page – not easily visible.

These 4 lines, starting with INPUT1, are used to show the numbers, by having different weights, for example:
A 1 mug block, 2 mug block, 4 mug block, 8 mug block. Added together, we have 15 again.

This means 0 and 15 mugs represented by 4 bits, see higher up: If we were to add another mug, then we would get the overflow as mentioned before, and the relevant register would be 0. Not allowed here. This simplified model excludes this option and any overflows are lost.

These 4 bits have the different weights 1 2 4 8 How can we memorize this easily?

One example might be to use a family:
10 years – a child
20 years - the adult
40 years - the parents
80 years – the grand parents
Might be a bit far fetched – but take the 0 away, and we have our weights 1 2 4 8 .

And add them together as 1 + 2 + 4 + 8 and we have again our number 15 – the maximum we can pack into our registers.

Next, we have to look at our recipee and follow the lines – in programming speak the program - with one instruction to be executed per line.
On the right you will see where needed the same instuction as a 2 digit number in shorthand.

Now we write a program to make a cup of coffee

It is rather simplified might seem far fetched, but explaining the process as a few steps, and translating it into the shorthand for our computer on the right hand side.

These Instruction Numbers are basically the y and x coordinates of the reduced Instruction Table on the next page.
The full Instruction Table will be explained in more detail in the book.

Our mugs from above have all been moved from where the were on the picture to the outside as ressource and to display numbers.

Reduced Instruction Table for the Example here

	0	1	2	3	4	5	6	7	8	9	A	B	C	D	E	F
	NOT USED HERE	NOT USED HERE	DELAY	Jump Back	LOAD A with	Register Transfer	Register Transfer		PAGE							
0									0							
1					1	A to B	B to A		1							
2					2	A to C	C to A		2							
3					3	A to D	D to A		3							
4					4	A to OUT	IN to A		4							
5					5				5							
6					6				6							
7					7				7							
8					8											
9					9											
A / 10																
B / 11																
C / 13																
D / 14																
E /14																
f / 15																

Our Instruction Set defines what is possible.

1. So, we need **a mug**.
   We have to define how many to take – here 1.
   We have to define where to put it. into register A

   So the first instruction is get one mug into register A.
   We write it in shorthand as (y =4 and x = 1) 4 1

2. **Regster A** is an important ressource, and often used.
   It is right in front of us and we use it for many other activities,
   so let us clear it and shift the mug to another one: **Register C.**

   We move it from Register A to **Register C** and the command is 5 2

3. Now we need **some coffee**,
   Let's assume we want later in our mug **5 gram** units.
   Register A had been freed, see above, so it means 5 units into **Register A** 4 5

4. Out from our main working **register A** as before, transfer to **D** via 5 3

5. Next we need some sugar **8 gram units**, into **Register A** 4 8
   And shift it from Register A to Register B via 5 1

6. And now 3 units of milk into **Register A** means 4 3

So what do we have on our table on the plates now?

R A = 3 g milk - RB = 8g sugar - R C = 1 mug - RD = 5g coffee

1 mug/unit	in register C
5 grams/units of coffee	in register D
8 grams/units sugar	in register B
3 grams/units of milk	in register A

Now start mixing, and we have to get the sequence right,
based on possibilities available, not all moves are asupported.

Register A is the important one, our working area

Add sugar to milk A <= A + B , frees register B 7 3

R A = 3 g milk - RB = 8g sugar - R C = 1 mug - RD = 5g coffee
+ 8g sugar

Add coffe to milk and sugar mix before

Not directly possible, maths via reg.A, and there is only A + B

So, first free register A B <= A 5 1

Now coffee from D to A A <= D 6 3

Now mix coffee to sugar and milk 7 3

R A = 3 g milk - **RB =** 8g sugar - **R C = 1 mug** - **RD =** 5g coffee
+ 8g sugar
+ 5g coffee

And again we have to free register A for further work

So, first free register A B <= A 5 1

Now mug from D to A A <= D 6 3

Put milk, sugar and coffee into the mug

Add to the mug milk, sugar and coffeesugar to milk <= A + B 7 3

Try to change the sequence where you put the parts to make it easier to add them.

So what is left is to add the water and to output it all from register A.

The rest is now an exercise:

Finally we have to add water
But how many units?

We start pouring and measure the height as it goes .
This is our INPUT
the maximum before the mug overflows is 9 units

So input one unit of hot water.
Where are we? 1
And 1 more, to 2, then 3, then 4, then 5,
then 6, then 7, then 8, then 9

Have we reached 9? if yes, then get out of the adding water loop.

This is where the **SKIP** instruction is used:
We SKIP over the adding one unit of water loop.

A quick description of SKIP:
It means taking a decision either to continue on a road straight forward
or turn off, based on a decision.
You either jump (SKIP) over the road that turns off and then goes underneath, or you follow the detour and follow another road.

If not reached yet, then add another unit and so on and stay in the loop.
Until 9 units have been added.
Now we have finished our coffee.

So output our mug via Dout <= A 5 4

This example has been kept very simple to understand
some points not 100% correct.

But it shows the different steps and some of our instructions.

Just make up your own examples to use the instructions available in a way more related to your real world.

The PAGE Register

There is one other point that has to be mentioned:

We have only 16 lines on each page to write our instructions on.
Then we have the overflow as explained before - from 1111 to 1 0000;
line 0 to line 15 / F.
The 16th line is overflowing, so we need another register that counts the pages.

Our **4 Bit Page Register**. Just imagine it as an additional 4 bits in front of our instruction line counter – or more correctly in computer speak – the Program Counter.
To fill these now 8 bits lets us count from line 00 to line FF hex = 255 decimal.
The first page as we start is called here page 0.

So, after 16 instructions have been written down, we end up on PAGE 1 and so on.
16 lines further we are on PAGE 2.
The maximum we are using here as shown in the table is 7 pages. There are other implemenations with more as you will learn in the book.

We have covered here just some instructions – and as you can see, not much different from our daily life.

Having gone through these basics, you can now go back to the beginning of this book and start reading.

We hope you enjoy reading this book
– or will try some programs on the simulator.

For any feedback, please leave a comment on amazon, or send a quick email to epldfpga@aol.com

Exeter, November 2018

The next 4 pages are just copied from page 115 onwards
and are placed again here if you want to cut them out
or copy them to have them handy.

9.1 The Simulator and the Row of Buttons

```
|-- EXIT the program
|  |-- CREATE a NEW program ( Control+N )
|  |  |-- OPEN a file ( Control+O )
|  |  |  |-- SAVE the actual program ( Control + S )
|  |  |  |  |-- ADD a new line to the program
|  |  |  |  |  |-- DELETE the actual line
|  |  |  |  |  |   |-- SHOW the actual programming file
|  |  |  |  |  |   |  |-- UPLOAD the program to the target ( Control+U )
|  |  |  |  |  |   |  |   |-- CREATE a HEX file
|  |  |  |  |  |   |  |   |  |-- EXECUTE a single instruction ( F5 )
|  |  |  |  |  |   |  |   |  |  |-- Execute the next step ( F8 )
|  |  |  |  |  |   |  |   |  |  |  |-- STOP the debug program execution ( F6 )
|  |  |  |  |  |   |  |   |  |  |  |  | -- START / STOP program execution ( F9)
|  |  |  |  |  |   |  |   |  |  |  |  |    |-SELECT target Holtek-Mega8-TINY84-Arduino
```

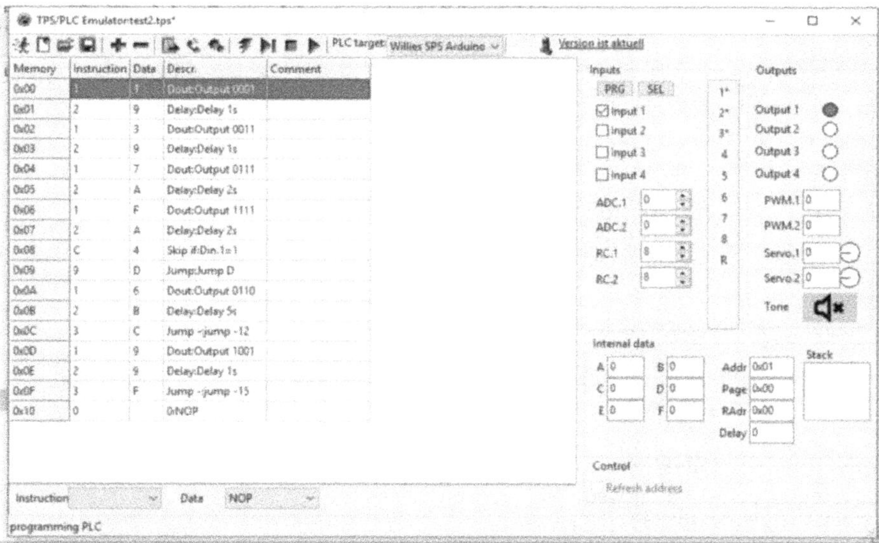

Memory: Showing the memory locations where the instructions are stored

Instruction: Instruction to be executed at the memory execution

Data: Data related to the instruction

Description: Automatically added description

Comment: Own comment to be added

Instruction: Instruction to be inserted into the current memory location

Data: Then open Data and select related number or function

9.2 - The Function Window - on the right hand side

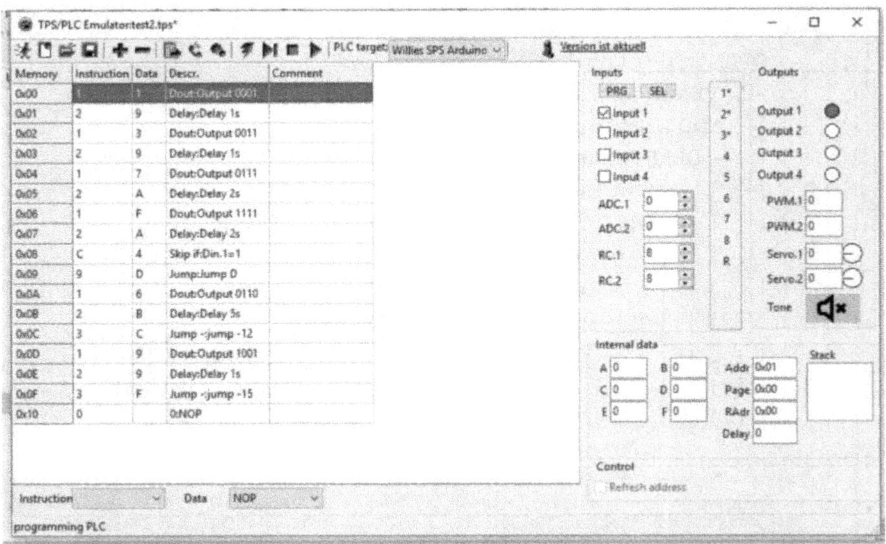

PRG / Program **SEL /** Select

INPUTS:

Input 1 – 4	The four inputs to be set by mouse click	
ADC 1, 2	Two simulated analog inputs	– input a number between 0 ... 255
RC1, 2	Two simulated RC servo outputs	– input a number between 0 ... 255

OUTPUTS:

Output 1 – 4	The four output bits sent by the PLC – Programmable Logic Controller
PWM 1, 2	Pulse Width Modulated outputs, an ON / OFF rectangular output signal
Servo 1, 2	RC servo outputs, simulating the angle by showing a number plus icon
Tone:	A sound to be output – to be added later

INTERNAL DATA of this PLC:
The inputs are fed via the instructions into registers
RA, RB, RC, RD, (RE, RF) and processed

Addr	The current memory location addressed
Page	Each memory block page consists of 16 locations, the page display changes accordingly And JUMPs will setting up a PAGE number if different
Radr	**RETURN ADDRESS** – if subroutine is called, return address is shown here

DELAY	Showing time is a delay instruction is executed
(SKIP	If a skip decision is executed, 1 indicates jump over next instruction **)** **tbd**

9.3 - Instruction Table

Instruction Set shaded in yellow aextensions of ArduinoSPS/ATTiny84 version.

	0	1	2	3	4	5	6	7
	n.n.	Port	Delay	Jump back rel	A=	„=A“	A=	A= Options
0	NOP	off	1ms	0	0	A<->B		
1		1	2ms	1	1	B=A	A=B	A=A + 1
2		2	5ms	2	2	C=A	A=C	A=A - 1
3		3	10ms	3	3	D=A	A=D	A=A + B
4		4	20ms	4	4	Dout=A	Din	A=A - B
5		5	50ms	5	5	Dout.0=A.0	Din.0	A=A * B
6		6	100ms	6	6	Dout.1=A.0	Din.1	A=A / B
7		7	200ms	7	7	Dout.2=A.0	Din.2	A=A and B
8		8	500ms	8	8	Dout.3=A.0	Din.3	A=A or B
9		9	1s	9	9	PWM.0=A	ADC.0	A=A xor B
a		10	2s	10	10	PWM.1=A	ADC.1	A= not A
b		11	5s	11	11	Servo.0=A	RCin.0	A= A % B (Rem.)
c		12	10s	12	12	Servo.1=A	RCin.1	A= A + 16 * B
d		13	20s	13	13	E=A	A=E	A= B - A
e		14	30s	14	14	F=A	A=F	
f		15	60s	15	15	Push A	Pop A	

8	9	a	b	c	d	e	f
Page	Jump absolute	C*	D*	Skip if	Call # + (16* Page)	Callsub /Ret	Byte Instr.
0	0	0	0	A=0	0	ret	A=ADC.0
1	1	1	1	A>B	1	Call 1	A=ADC.1
2	2	2	2	A<B	2	2	A=RCin.0
3	3	3	3	A=B	3	3	A=RCin.1
4	4	4	4	Din.0=1	4	4	PWM.0=A
5	5	5	5	Din.1=1	5	5	PWM.1=A
6	6	6	6	Din.2=1	6	6	Servo.0=A
7	7	7	7	Din.3=1	7		Servo.1=A
8	8	8	8	Din.0=0	8	Def 1	
9	9	9	9	Din.1=0	9	2	
10	10	10	10	Din.2=0	10	3	
11	11	11	11	Din.3=0	11	4	
12	12	12	12	S_PRG=0	12	5	
13	13	13	13	S_SEL=0	13	6	
14	14	14	14	S_PRG=1	14		
15	15	15	15	S_SEL=1	15	restart	PrgEnd

9.4 - TPS / SPS Emulator

http://wkla.no-ip.biz/ArduinoWiki/doku.php?id=arduino:arduinosps:spsemu

Switch top left to English if needed. Copied from Willie's website

For the TPS PLC (and my extensions) I once wrote an emulator as a fun project. Here the result.

The complete project is programmed in Lazarus (Freepascal).

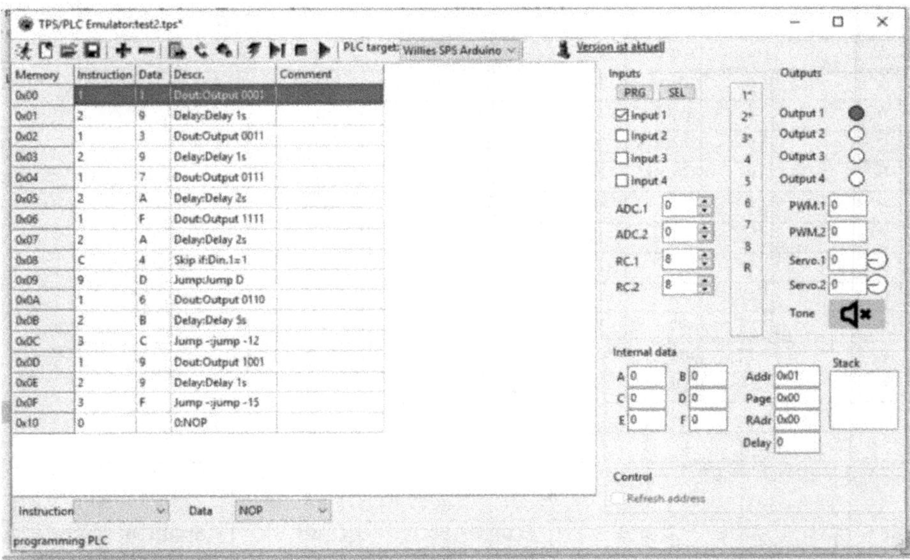

The emulator can work with the different instruction sets of different TPS versions. On the left you can see the programming window.

This can either be typed in directly or generated via the two combo boxes below.

There you can select the possible commands – dependent on the target selected of the included versions.

The commands can then be executed via the 4 buttons in the top center block.

The first button tests the currently selected command (jumps are not carried out)

The second button executes the program in single-step mode.

The third button stops single-step mode

The fourth button is Start-Stop, to run at maximum speed.

In the left window you make the entries and view the results as you step through the program.

www.ingramcontent.com/pod-product-compliance
Lightning Source LLC
LaVergne TN
LVHW041204050326
832903LV00020B/451

* 9 7 8 1 7 3 1 2 3 2 5 3 3 *